LIGUORI CHRISTIAN INITIATION

M000228018

Journey of Faith

FOR TEENS

ENLIGHTENMENT AND MYSTAGOGY LEADER GUIDE

Liguori
PUBLICATIONS
A Redemptorist Ministry

Journey of Faith for Teens Enlightenment and Mystagogy Leader Guide (827150)

Imprimi Potest: Stephen T. Rehrauer, CSsR, Provincial, Denver Province, the Redemptorists

Imprimatur: "In accordance with CIC 827, permission to publish has been granted on December 12, 2016, by the Rev. Msgr. Mark S. Rivituso, Vicar General, Archdiocese of St. Louis. Permission to publish is an indication that nothing contrary to Church teaching is contained in this work. It does not imply any endorsement of the opinions expressed in the publication; nor is any liability assumed by this permission."

Text: Adapted from *Journey of Faith for Adults* © 2000 Liguori Publications.

Editor of 2016 edition: Theresa Nienaber. Design: Lorena Mitre Jimenez. Images: Shutterstock.

Printed in the United States of America.
20 19 18 17 16 / 5 4 3 2 1
Third Edition

Contents

Enlightenment and Mystagogy: A Review

Enlightenment Lesson Plans

Mystagogy Lesson Plans

Enlightenment and Mystagogy Glossary

Enlightenment and Mystagogy: A Review

The Period of Purification and Enlightenment

Since the earliest centuries, the Church has set aside the season of Lent as a particular time for repentance, conversion, and preparation for the sacraments. The RCIA process and celebration of baptism is centered on the Easter Vigil, with the rites of election and calling, scrutinies, and entire catechumenate scheduled in relation to that feast (RCIA 17, 20–26; CCC 1168; CIC 856).

Because repentance and conversion require personal and internal preparation, the *Journey of Faith for Teens, Enlightenment* lessons focus on guided, prayerful reflection. The lessons will assist the participants in their internal preparation for the sacraments, and encourage them to live out their faith in hands-on ways.

"[Enlightenment] is a period of more intense spiritual preparation, consisting more in interior reflection than in catechetical instruction, and is intended to purify the minds and hearts of the elect as they search their own consciences and do penance" *(RCIA 139)*.

While the elect do not fully possess the graces and gifts of discipleship during the period of purification and enlightenment, they should feel ownership of their Christian faith. Baptized candidates, as members of the Christian Church, should begin to identify themselves as Catholic and express their faith in keeping with sacred Tradition.

The sessions and events during the enlightenment period should enable participants to experience Lent along with the parish community, who is also undergoing spiritual renewal and preparing to celebrate the paschal mystery more deeply (RCIA 138). At the Easter Vigil, the faithful will renew their baptismal vows as the participants profess their faith in Christ and the Catholic Church. This unity and integration will grow throughout the period of mystagogy, which usually corresponds to the Easter season.

Rites and Sacraments During the Period of Enlightenment

The enlightenment and purification period begins with the rite of election. Please refer to the *Catechumenate Leader Guide* and other *Journey of Faith for Teens* materials for details.

The Scrutinies

Rather than examination, interrogation, or harsh judgment, "the scrutinies...are rites for self-searching and repentance," designed "to inspire in the elect a desire for purification and redemption" (RCIA 141, 143). The prayers and intercessions encourage the elect to strive for the narrow gate (Matthew 7:13–14; Luke 13:24–28). Through the exorcisms, they "are freed from the effects of sin and from the influence of the devil" (RCIA 144). Having previously been instructed in the nature of sin and expressed their desire and commitment to receive the sacraments of initiation, participants are strengthened and sent forth to make their discipleship a reality.

The questions, activities, journal prompts, and other material in these guides help to prepare each participant for this stage in their faith journey. The bishop or priest will "question the candidates individually" in the formula for the profession of faith at the Easter Vigil (RCIA 224–25). Should a participant express doubts or concerns about their conversion, meet with him or her privately to determine what additional support can be provided.

The Presentations

The *Presentation of the Creed* should be celebrated during the week following the first scrutiny and, whenever possible, within a Mass so that the faith community may be present (RCIA 157; CIC 837). It prepares the elect to memorize the Creed, for the *Recitation of the Creed* (see Preparation Rites), and to profess their faith on the day of their baptism (RCIA 148).

During the *Presentation of the Creed*:

- The prescribed readings, which replace the regular weekday readings, are proclaimed during the Liturgy of the Word (RCIA 158).

- After the homily, the priest calls the elect forward to receive the words and mysteries of the Creed. The Nicene or Apostles' Creed may be used, depending on the parish's tradition (RCIA 160).

- The priest begins to recite the Creed and the assembly joins in.

- The priest prays over the elect and dismisses them prior to the Liturgy of the Eucharist. If they are to stay, he reminds them that they cannot participate fully, but that they remain "as a sign of our hope that all God's children will eat and drink with the Lord..." (RCIA 163).

The *Presentation of the Lord's Prayer* should be celebrated during the week following the third scrutiny or in the preparation rites. It prepares the elect to make the prayer their own as they join the congregation in praying it before their first Eucharist (*RCIA* 149).

During the *Presentation of the Lord's Prayer*:

- The prescribed readings, which replace the regular weekday readings, are proclaimed during the Liturgy of the Word (*RCIA* 179).

- Just prior to the Gospel reading, the deacon or assisting minister calls the elect forward. Matthew's Gospel account of the Lord's Prayer is proclaimed.

- After the homily, the priest prays over the elect: "Deepen the faith and understanding of these elect, chosen for baptism. Give them new birth…so that they may be numbered among your adopted children" (*RCIA* 182).

- The priest dismisses the elect prior to the Liturgy of the Eucharist.

Preparation Rites on Holy Saturday

The number and arrangement of these rites will depend on the needs of your elect, timing and ability, and other factors (*RCIA* 185–86). The Church offers the following model for your benefit (*RCIA* 187–92):

1. Begin with an appropriate gathering song.

2. The celebrant greets everyone with a suitable formula or words.

3. Scripture readings are chosen from the rites and proclaimed, with psalms or hymns in between, if needed.

4. The celebrant gives a brief homily or explanation of the texts.

5. The various rites are celebrated. These may include the *Presentation of the Lord's Prayer,* the *Recitation of the Creed,* the *Ephphetha Rite,* and/ or the rite of *Choosing a Baptismal Name.*

6. The celebrant concludes with the prayer of blessing and dismissal.

The Easter Vigil

The feast of Easter, in particular the Easter Vigil liturgy, is the highlight of the Church year. Given its prominence and his prerogative to initiate (baptize) those fourteen years old or older, the bishop is the preferred celebrant (RCIA 207; CIC 863). "Adult candidates, including children of catechetical age, are to receive baptism, confirmation, and eucharist in a single eucharistic celebration" (National Statutes for the Catechumenate, 14). This trifecta of sacraments is a distinct feature of the RCIA process and reflects the unified nature of Christian initiation (CIC 842).

If a mixed group of the elect and baptized candidates are to celebrate the sacraments together, "the condition and status of those already baptized should be carefully respected and distinguished" (*National Statutes* 26, 33–34). Whenever this is the case, your RCIA process should reflect the difference between these two groups from the beginning. Continuing it through the Easter Vigil should not be hard. The bishop or priest may already have solutions.

The Vigil Mass and sacraments of initiation are discussed in the *Journey of Faith Inquiry Leader Guide,* lesson C1: *The RCIA Process and Rites,* and lesson E7: *The Meaning of Holy Week.* You may also refer to *RCIA* 206–43 and *Lectionary* no. 41. Additional steps and points are detailed here:

- The celebration of baptism begins with a presentation of the elect with their godparents, and a litany of the saints.

- The celebrant blesses and prays over the baptismal waters.

- The elect renounce sin and make a profession of faith. "Adults are not saved unless they come forward of their own accord and with the will to accept God's gift through their own belief. The faith of those to be baptized is not simply the faith of the Church, but the personal faith of each one of them…" (*RCIA* 211).

- The elect are baptized, preferably by immersion (*National Statutes* 17). Whether baptism is by full or partial immersion or simply by pouring, it should "take on its full importance as the sign of that mystical sharing in Christ's death and resurrection through which those who believe in his name die to sin and rise to eternal life….This washing is not a mere purification rite but the sacrament of being joined to Christ" (*RCIA* 213).

- The newly baptized are anointed with oil and clothed in a white garment. Godparents are presented with a candle lit from the Easter candle.

- The celebrant invites the newly baptized to receive confirmation. Afterward, the assembled faithful renew their baptismal promises. If the combined rite is used, the renewal will come first, followed by confirmation.

- Now previously baptized candidates come forward and profess their faith. The sacrament of confirmation is conferred with the laying on of hands and anointing with chrism.

- As the Liturgy of the Eucharist begins, neophytes should take part in the procession of the gifts to the altar (*RCIA* 241). The entire RCIA group and its supporters—neophytes, leaders, catechists, sponsors, godparents, and family members—should receive the Eucharist under both forms (*RCIA* 243, 594).

Practical Suggestions

- Prepare the RCIA team, participants, sponsors, and godparents for the rites of sending, election, and/or calling prior to the beginning of Lent. If Lent is early, you may have to adjust the catechumenate period accordingly. Lesson E1: *Election: Saying Yes to Jesus* is specifically designed for this purpose.

- Help the elect and candidates enter the Lenten season as deeply as possible. Present lesson E2: *Living Lent* early in the season. It provides a context and offers suggestions for the season. Attend the Ash Wednesday service as an RCIA group and incorporate Lenten readings, themes, prayers, and sacramentals into the sessions. Distribute a daily Lenten devotional or activity and encourage godparents and sponsors to discuss it with participants regularly.

- Arrange a time in the church, chapel, or a nearby shrine where the RCIA group can pray, even walk, the stations together using lesson E5: *The Way of the Cross.* Assign individuals to announce the stations, proclaim the Scriptures, and read the reflections and prayers aloud.

- Schedule the remaining enlightenment lessons to correspond with their respective rites or celebrations. Present lesson E3: *Scrutinies: Looking Within* before the third Sunday of Lent and lessons E4: *The Creed* and E6: *The Lord's Prayer* before the presentations. Lesson E7: *The Meaning of Holy Week* can be presented on or before Palm Sunday. Lesson *E8: Easter Vigil Retreat* should be presented as close to the Easter Vigil as possible.

- Arrange a special celebration of reconciliation for the baptized candidates prior to the Easter Vigil (*National Statutes* 27). Whether these individuals are non-Catholics celebrating their first penance or uncatechized Catholics returning to the sacrament after many years, make sure they receive proper preparation, instruction, and support. Strongly encourage their leaders, catechists, sponsors, godparents, and baptized family and friends to attend as well. If the group is large, it may be better to schedule this event separately from regular reconciliation times.

- During the Easter Vigil, baptized candidates should come forward for confirmation after the baptism of the elect is completed. Have previously baptized candidates stand together, to distinguish their different sacramental status.

- Celebrate with the parish community after the Easter Vigil or during the Easter octave, but reserve any closing or final celebrations for after mystagogy (Pentecost) to reflect the unfinished nature of the RCIA process at Easter. Incorporate the communal, covenantal, and evangelistic themes of Pentecost into your festivities. (See *RCIA* 249.)

The Period of Postbaptismal Catechesis or Mystagogy

The words *mystagogy* and *mystery* share a Greek root meaning "initiated person." With this last period of the RCIA process, the Church recognizes the need for continuing and deepening support for the newly baptized. Although they have been formed and converted, there is still much to learn from the Church and the full experience of Catholic living: "The faith required for Baptism is not a perfect or mature faith, but a beginning that is called to develop....For all the baptized, children or adults, faith must grow *after* Baptism" (*CCC* 1253–54; see also *RCIA* 245).

The Church sets aside the Easter season as the ideal time to delve into the mysteries of our faith, the sacraments, and the Church (*RCIA* 247). During these fifty days, the Sunday liturgies should specially focus on the new members of the body of Christ, and the people of the parish should extend themselves in welcoming their new brothers and sisters. The readings from the Acts of the Apostles emphasize the community and the continuing work of salvation through the ever-growing discipleship of the fledgling Church.

The mystagogy sessions should facilitate the neophytes' full participation in the sacraments and integration into the faith community. "This is a time for the community and the neophytes together to grow in deepening their grasp of the paschal mystery and in making it part of their lives through meditation on the Gospel, sharing in the eucharist, and doing the works of charity" (*RCIA* 244). By their shared presence and fervor, they witness to the joy of the gospel and serve as examples of living disciples.

Effective Catechesis During Mystagogy

In his apostolic exhortation On Catechesis in Our Time (*Catechesi Tradendae),* Pope St. John Paul II identifies several elements of catechesis. Three of them are fundamental to the period of mystagogy: "celebration of the sacraments, integration into the ecclesial community, and apostolic and missionary witness" (*CT* 18; see *CCC* 6). To that Pope Francis added some practical demands of what he called *"mystagogic* initiation" (the Joy of the Gospel [*Evangelii Gaudium*], 166). These guidelines provide a framework from which you can build a meaningful period of postbaptismal catechesis:

- *Create a suitable environment.* Give your sessions a distinctly liturgical feel. Incorporate sacred art, music, and liturgical prayers, texts, and forms whether or not they are connected to Sunday Mass.

- *Offer an attractive presentation.* Continue to emphasize the beauty of our faith and to explore how what we do reflects the joyful hope of Christ's death and resurrection.

- *Continue the use of eloquent symbols.* Connect the liturgy and sacraments to the wonders of nature, human nature and daily life, and the participants' own experiences to deepen their meaning and value.

- *Include the process in a broader growth process.* Emphasize that in baptism we have died to our old selves and risen to a new life. The mystagogy lessons are designed to prompt the neophytes to active discipleship.

- *Focus on evangelization rather than instruction.* Remind everyone (including yourself) that the light of faith is present. After baptism, your job is to fan the Spirit's flame. Incorporate more listening and sharing of experiences into your sessions. When discussing Scripture, go beyond understanding the story and prompt each person to make it his or her own.

- *Provide opportunities for contemplation and discernment.* Plan a prayer session or visit to the adoration chapel. Dedicate at least part of a session to reflecting on the Triduum and Vigil in particular. Spend ten to twenty minutes each week on the lesson questions and journal prompts.

- *Guide the participants toward greater initiative.* If you haven't already, teach participants to lead simple prayers and to proclaim Scripture. Encourage them to share how God is working in their lives and to determine ways in which they can respond.

Transitioning Into the Parish Community

Through the sacraments of initiation, the neophytes are permanently changed (*CCC* 1272). With their newfound grace, salvation, and identity, they receive the responsibilities of discipleship and call to active participation in parish life. Yet the mysteries of the Easter Vigil impact the Church as well (*RCIA* 246). In the liturgy and reception of new members, it is refreshed, made new. The period of mystagogy is a time for neophytes and the rest of the faithful to welcome each other and to discern where God is leading them together.

As primary representatives of the community, RCIA leaders and catechists must model this new relationship and extend it to the rest of the parish and diocese. Some ways to start include making introductions, encouraging the neophytes' full participation in the Mass, and supporting their early efforts to carry the gospel to others in word, deed, and ministry.

Ways to Create Community

- *Recognize the neophytes and newly received by name.* Make the assembly aware of their presence in the community. Consider common mentions of other groups, such as the sick, recently deceased, and baptized infants. Follow your pastor or parish leader's instructions for requesting a special intention or spoken or written announcement.

- *Bring the Mass to them.* The Sundays of Easter are "so-called Masses for neophytes" (*RCIA* 247). This doesn't require a teaching Mass or special treatment, but they should be able to see the deep, spiritual realities happening in and around them. Having the neophytes sit together or focusing the homily on the sacraments can help.

- *Keep the Easter season.* Rather than wind down after the Easter Vigil, work with the pastor and the whole parish to take part in the ongoing marvels of Easter.

- *Create spiritual connections.* Post or print questions or material from your sessions where parishioners can access them. This gives them an experience of mystagogy and a convenient way to share reflections and discussions with their own families.

- *Allow for gradual integration.* Invite godparents, sponsors, and family to continue attending Mass with the neophytes and assisting them in their ongoing formation. Regularly exploring the parish bulletin, newsletter, or social-media feed together for events to attend is a simple activity that can be done over coffee or brunch.

As the participants approach their first sacramental anniversary, you may observe the fruits of established friendships, familiarity, and a real commitment to the faith. In turn, the Church gives thanks and offers these gifts for the benefit of all, including a new group of neophytes.

Catechism: 422–429

Objectives

- Compare reactions to Jesus' life and teachings throughout the Gospels and history.

- Connect Jesus' universal invitation to discipleship to the signing of the *Book of the Elect* in the rite of election.

- Practice self-examination.

Leader Meditation

John 21:1–19

Jesus Christ has made you a fisher of young men and women. The participants in your class are the fish in your net, the net you dropped at the Lord's command, the net you hauled up and have carried to shore. It is time to present the fish to the Lord. The Lord asks Peter if Peter loves him. The first time Peter says "yes," Jesus tells Peter to feed the Lord's lambs. The second time, the Lord tells Peter to tend to the Lord's sheep. The third time, the Lord says to Peter to feed his sheep. In doing these things, Peter will act on his love for Jesus Christ. You are like Peter. You will bring the sheep to the Lord, and he will invite them to say "yes" to him. Pray for the necessary grace to lead the participants well and for sufficient grace that they will respond with a firm "yes."

Leader Preparation

- Read the lesson handout, this lesson plan, the Scripture passage, and *Catechism* sections.

- Be familiar with the vocabulary terms for this lesson: discipleship, testimony, *Book of the Elect*. Definitions are provided in this guide's glossary.

Welcome

Greet participants as they arrive. Check for supplies and immediate needs. Solicit questions or comments about the previous session and/or share new information and findings. Begin promptly.

Opening Scripture

John 21:1–19

Ask a volunteer to light the candle and read aloud. Share with participants that this lesson is all about Jesus inviting us to become his disciples. He is offering us the opportunity to say yes to him, to do his will, and to love his people. Before beginning your discussion of the lesson handout, ask participants **what it means to truly be one of Jesus' disciples.**

> "From this loving knowledge of Christ springs the desire to proclaim him, to 'evangelize,' and to lead others to the 'yes' of faith in Jesus Christ."
>
> *CCC 428*

Journey of Faith

In Short:

- Christians have reacted in many ways to Jesus' message of discipleship throughout history.
- As members of the elect, you are called to discipleship.
- As you grow in your faith, you will be asked to engage in self-examination.

Election: Saying "Yes" to Jesus

Maria is twenty years old and the mother of an active two-year-old boy. She works forty hours a week but still struggles to make ends meet. She left high school during her senior year.

Maria's parents begged her to remain in school, and her favorite teacher tried to convince her of the benefits of hitting the books and toughing it out. But Maria wasn't convinced. Working in the real world seemed to be the smartest choice. She'd still learn, but she'd also be making money and getting work experience.

Now Maria is beginning to wonder what would have happened if she'd said "yes" to finishing high school. It will be difficult to go back to school now that she's a mom with more adult responsibilities, but she feels called to say "yes" to this opportunity now. It won't be easy, but she still has her family's support for a new life experience she knows will help her.

> • Have you ever said "no" to something only to find yourself saying "yes" to it later? Briefly describe the situation and what changed.

Jesus invited many to become his disciples and to carry on his mission after him. As the Gospels tell us, many responded enthusiastically—including some Galilean fishermen, tax collectors, and women. People from every walk of life accepted Jesus' call to come and follow him.

Not everyone said "yes" to Jesus, though. **Discipleship**—being a follower of Jesus—isn't easy. It requires a big commitment and saying "yes" to things not everyone was ready for. While being a follower of Jesus comes with all the blessings of eternal life, it's a decision that can't be made without some understanding of what it means. It's better for us to give an authentic, thoughtful "yes" to God than a halfhearted "yes" that means we just go through the motions.

> • Can you think of some reasons people give for saying 'no' to their faith? Why did you choose to say 'yes?'

Rite of Election: An Opportunity for Commitment

"From this loving knowledge of Christ springs the desire to proclaim him...to lead others to the 'yes,' of faith in Jesus Christ. But at the same time the need to know this faith better makes itself felt."

CCC 429

CCC 422–429

Rite of Election: An Opportunity for Commitment

- Ask participants to think about how they've responded to God's call in their lives so far. If you have time, share your own experience of saying yes (or no) to God's call as you grew in your faith.

- Discuss as a group why some people may say "not yet" to God's call. Use the story of St. Peter as an example; why did Peter deny God only to give a wholehearted yes later.

Suggested responses may include: We may not fully understand our faith yet, we may be letting a bad experience with a person influence how we see faith, we may secretly be afraid of what happens if we say yes, etc.

Election: Saying Yes to Jesus

- Give participants a chance to read the introduction to the lesson handout on their own and think about their answer to the reflection question. Ask any participants who feel comfortable sharing to do so. Think about this reflection question yourself and share any relevant experience with the group.

- Discuss what it means to be a disciple and why true discipleship might be difficult in today's world.

Suggested responses include: Pressure to fit in with secular society, fear of being made fun of, fear of standing out or being singled out, etc.

- Discuss the reflection question together. Emphasize to participants that while faith does not require total understanding, and isn't measured by our understanding, we can't give a wholehearted "yes" to a faith we don't understand in any way.

"I will, but first…"

- Discuss with participants why it's tempting to tell God "yes, but first…."

- Ask participants why we shouldn't wait to give God our "yes."

Suggested responses may include: The timing may never be perfect, like the apostles we have to serve God where we are, God may be calling us where we are for a reason, etc.

"Some of Jesus' teachings are just too hard to follow."

- If you have time, read the story of the Samaritan woman in full (John 4:4–42). Discuss with participants what about Jesus' message would have been easy to say yes to and what would have been difficult.

Suggested responses include: He promises the woman living water, he proves he is a prophet and offers her salvation, he asks her to give up the beliefs she's known, he asks her to go out and tell others about him.

On the first Sunday of Lent or close to the beginning of Lent, the catechumens celebrate the rite of election. Election comes from a word that means choose, and the whole ceremony reflects this theme. God has chosen us and called us. How have you responded to that call?

After the Church community hears **testimony**, that is, public statements from the catechumens and their sponsors on how the catechumens have chosen to respond to God's call, the community is then asked to accept those catechumens who are ready to receive the sacraments. The catechumens say "yes" by stating their desire to join the Church and then writing their names in the **Book of the Elect**.

The rite of election begins the stage of purification and enlightenment, the final stage of the journey for catechumens and candidates. You've asked questions about the Church, and you've become part of the community. Now it's time for you to examine your life and to think about what Christ asks of you.

At the time of Jesus, some said "yes" to his call, while others said, "no, not yet." What made the difference?

Today Christ has called you. How will you respond? As you reflect on what it means to be a disciple of Jesus, have you ever used any of the following excuses when you felt Jesus' call?

"I will, but first…"

> *"Desire for true happiness frees man from his immoderate attachment to the goods of this world so that he can find his fulfillment in the vision and beatitude of God."*
>
> *CCC 2548*

The Gospels of Matthew and Luke both describe Jesus' invitation to potential disciples who say they desire to follow him but not just yet: "Lord, let me go first and bury my father" (Matthew 8:21). In Jesus' time, this meant "let me come after my father is dead." In Luke's Gospel, the hesitant disciple says, "I will follow you, Lord, but first let me say farewell to my family at home" (Luke 9:61).

To us, Jesus' response may seem cold and harsh: "Let the dead bury their dead….No one who sets a hand to the plow and looks to what was left behind is fit for the kingdom of God" (Luke 9:60,62). But what the Gospel writer is trying to tell us is that we can't follow Christ only when it fits into our schedule. We aren't true disciples of Jesus if we live as disciples only when it's safe and convenient. We have to follow the Lord's commands when we're out with our friends and when we're at home with our parents. True followers of Christ aren't part-time, only-when-no-one's-looking disciples.

When we accept Jesus' call we must do so enthusiastically, making it our top priority. The Galilean fishermen "left everything and followed him" (Luke 5:11). Matthew, the tax collector, "leaving everything behind, he got up and followed him" (Luke 5:28). Our family, relationships, hobbies, and activities, all take on their true meaning in our lives only when following Christ is our first priority.

"Some of Jesus' teachings are just too hard to follow."

> *"The more one does what is good, the freer one becomes. There is no true freedom except in the service of what is good and just."*
>
> *CCC 1733*

When Jesus spoke to the Samaritan woman at the well, he said many things that would have been hard for her to hear (John 4:18). But Jesus promised her "living water" that would keep her from ever thirsting again.

The Samaritan woman could have reacted with embarrassment, resentment, or anger. Jesus was asking her to radically change her life. But she didn't get upset or defensive. She ran back to her town to tell people Jesus was the Messiah. While the truth is often difficult for us to hear, we, like the Samaritan woman, must be open to receiving it.

"But I have so much stuff."

Of all Jesus' conversations with would-be disciples, maybe the one we can relate to best is the one with the rich young man who asked, "'Good teacher, what must I do to inherit eternal life?...' Jesus, looking at him, loved him and said to him, 'You are lacking in one thing. Go, sell what you have, and give to [the] poor and you will have treasure in heaven; then come, follow me.' At that statement his face fell, and he went away sad, for he had many possessions" (Mark 10:17–22).

In this conversation, Jesus is telling us that it's not good to become too attached to things. If we look to our stuff for happiness, we will always be aching for something more, something that really matters.

The rich young man couldn't let go of the false security of his possessions. He wasn't sure that he would find in Jesus, and within himself, something more valuable than his wealth.

This story challenges us to ask ourselves, "What things do I hold on to that may keep me from following the Lord? What do I own that is more important to me than God? More important than other people?"

"I do not know him."

Probably the saddest loss for Jesus came when, after his arrest, his closest friends ran away. Peter, who had sworn he would die with Jesus, denied three times that he even knew Jesus.

Many of Jesus' disciples thought he would lead Israel to glory and bring about an earthly kingdom. They weren't prepared for the truth of the cross.

It's easy to understand how frightened they were! None of the Twelve, except perhaps John, attended Jesus' crucifixion or burial. Just when Jesus needed them the most, they ran away and locked themselves in a room because they were afraid.

But not everyone ran in fear. "Standing by the cross of Jesus were his mother and his mother's sister, Mary the wife of Clopas, and Mary of Magdala" (John 19:25). No matter what the danger, these women stayed by Jesus. These brave women stayed by him and later went out to the tomb to anoint his body (Matthew 28:1–10).

> • Is it easier for you to follow Jesus when it's the popular decision or your prayers are being answered the way you expect? Why?
>
> • Have you ever said "no" to a cross Jesus asked you to bear? Why? Is it a decision you'd change if you could?

Our Response to Jesus' Call

Jesus must have felt very sad as he listened to all these excuses, as he watched all the would-be disciples turn and leave him. Many of them almost said "yes," but out of fear or attachment to things, they said "no" to the only one who could give lasting purpose and direction to their lives.

Our prayers and practices during Lent help us discover the strengths and weaknesses of our own responses to Christ's call. There is a little bit of the *would-be* disciple in each of us. It's difficult to give an unconditional "yes" to Christ—to embrace the cross that he asks us to carry with him. But Jesus didn't abandon his disciples. He sent them the graces they needed to say yes again. God won't force us into discipleship, but he will answer when we say, "yes, but help!"

"But I have so much stuff."

- Discuss with participants why it's difficult to let go of material security.

Suggested responses include: We feel secure when we have lots of physical things, material success is judged on how much money or stuff we have, etc.

- Discuss with participants why we need to let go of this false security before saying "yes" to God.

Suggested responses include: We have to trust in God as our security, we can't be attached to things of this earth, etc.

"I do not know him."

- Give participants time to answer the reflection questions on their own.

- If you have time, ask participants why fear may cause people, like St. Peter, to deny their faith.

With a partner or as a group, list as many excuses for following Jesus as you can think of in two minutes. Then pick a gift or fruit of the Holy Spirit that helps overcome that excuse, and explain how. (Gifts and fruits of the Holy Spirit are listed in sections 1831–32 of the *CCC*.)

Suggested responses include:

An attachment to earthly goods and possessions could be countered by generosity.

Frustration that God is taking too long to answer our prayers could be countered by patience.

With a partner or as a group, list as many excuses for following Jesus as you can think of in two minutes. Then pick a gift or fruit of the Holy Spirit that helps overcome that excuse, and explain how. (Gifts and fruits of the Holy Spirit are listed in sections 1831–32 of the *CCC*.)

What keeps you from following Christ more completely or consistently? Use the excuses discussed in the lesson to help you evaluate yourself as honestly as possible.

Journey of Faith for Teens: Enlightenment, E1 (826313)
Imprimi Potest: Stephen T. Rehrauer, CSsR, Provincial, Denver Province, the Redemptorists.
Imprimatur: "In accordance with CIC 827, permission to publish has been granted on June 30, 2016, by the Rev. Msgr. Mark S. Rivituso, Vicar General, Archdiocese of St. Louis. Permission to publish is an indication that nothing contrary to Church teaching is contained in this work. It does not imply any endorsement of the opinions expressed in the publication; nor is any liability assumed by this permission."
Journey of Faith for Teens © 2000, 2016 Liguori Publications, Liguori, MO 63057. All rights reserved. No part of this publication may be reproduced, distributed, stored, transmitted, or posted in any form by any means without prior written permission. To order, visit Liguori.org or call 800-325-9521. Liguori Publications, a nonprofit corporation, is an apostolate of the Redemptorists. To learn more about the Redemptorists, visit Redemptorists.com. Editors of 2016 edition: Theresa Nienaber and Pat Fosarelli, MD, DMin. Design: Lorena Mitre Jimenez. Images: Shutterstock.
Scripture texts in this work are taken from the *New American Bible*, revised edition © 2010, 1991, 1986, 1970 Confraternity of Christian Doctrine, Washington, D.C., and are used by permission of the copyright owner. All Rights Reserved. No part of the *New American Bible* may be reproduced in any form without permission in writing from the copyright owner. Excerpts from English translation of the *Catechism of the Catholic Church for the United States of America* © 1994 United States Catholic Conference, Inc.—Libreria Editrice Vaticana; English translation of the *Catechism of the Catholic Church: Modifications from the Editio Typica* © 1997 United States Catholic Conference, Inc.—Libreria Editrice Vaticana. Compliant with *The Roman Missal, Third Edition*.
Printed in the United States of America. 20 19 18 17 16 / 5 4 3 2 1. Third Edition.

ISBN 978-0-7648-2631-3

Liguori PUBLICATIONS
A Redemptorist Ministry

Journaling

What keeps you from following Christ more completely or consistently? Use the excuses discussed in the lesson to help you evaluate yourself as honestly as possible.

Closing Prayer

End with a few moments of silence and ask for petitions. Close with this prayer:

Lord, God our Father,
It is a blessing to know that you are our Lord, Creator, and Savior. You love us with an eternal love. It's difficult to comprehend this kind of love. You have given us the gift of free will, knowing that we may choose to walk away from you or we may choose to receive this love and say yes to it. Give us the grace to say yes, for it's our heart's desire to love you, to know you, and to serve you. Amen.

Take-Home

Ask participants to really think about their response to the journal prompt this lesson and spend the time between now and the next session to try and turn any "not yets" into "yeses."

E2: Living Lent

Catechism: 571–605, 1434–1439

Objectives

- Outline the historical foundation for the season of Lent.

- Identify the major themes of Lent: repentance, sacrifice, overcoming temptation, and spiritual growth.

- Recall the three Lenten practices of fasting, prayer, and almsgiving.

- List Lenten symbols or objects such as ashes, palms, purple, etc.

Leader Meditation

Matthew 4:1–11

Recall times when you have felt you were in a desert—times that were difficult and seemingly lifeless. Why are these the times we are most tempted to turn away from Christ and look for comfort elsewhere? In what places or in what things have you been tempted to find comfort? What brought you back to Christ?

Leader Preparation

- Read the lesson, this lesson plan, the Scripture passage, and the *Catechism* sections.

- Any physical symbols of Lent to show participants (ashes, palm leaves, images of the stations of the cross, etc.)

- Be familiar with the vocabulary terms for this lesson: fasting, abstinence. Definitions are provided in this guide's glossary.

Welcome

Greet participants as they arrive. Check for supplies and immediate needs. Solicit questions or comments about the previous session and/or share new information and findings. Begin promptly.

Opening Scripture

Matthew 4:1–11

Ask for a volunteer to light the candle and read aloud. Ask participants to think about their own desert experiences, and if they felt a stronger pull toward temptation during these times.

> "The event of the Cross and Resurrection abides and draws everything toward life."
>
> CCC 1085

Journey of Faith

In Short:

- The major themes of Lent include: repentance, sacrifice, growth, and overcoming temptation.
- The practices of fasting, prayer, and almsgiving are central to Lent.
- Many symbols are associated with Lent.

Living Lent

We take time to prepare for things that are important to us.

If you value earning good grades in school, you take time to prepare for major tests. If your goal is to make the soccer team, you prepare for tryouts by practicing. If you have an important role in the school play, you put hours into rehearsal. You will prepare for your future career by working hard in school and attending a college or technical school that will give you the best possible training and education.

- *What are some other things you prepare for?*
- *Why is preparation important?*

During Lent, we prepare for the greatest celebration of the Church year—Easter. We follow the path of Jesus, who journeyed through his death to his resurrection.

While Lent is a time of serious reflection, it's a positive time, too. The Church teaches that Lent is a time of preparation; a time of spiritual growth. Lent and Easter are a lot like spring: New attitudes and fresh ways of looking at things are born. Old attitudes and unhealthy habits disappear. The dying and rebirth of nature and the dying and rebirth that takes place within our hearts reflects the great mystery of the death and resurrection of our Lord.

For you during the RCIA, Lent is also a time of purification and enlightenment, a time when you are called to respond to God with greater reflection and commitment.

Why Forty Days?

The season of Lent is the Church's preparation for Easter, a liturgical season of forty days. The number forty plays a key role in several passages of both the Old Testament and the New Testament. The number forty isn't always literal and can be symbolic of any long period of trials or tests in the Bible.

How is forty used in the following passages?	
Genesis 7:17–18	Exodus 34:27–29
Matthew 4:1–4	Acts 1:1–5

The Gospels of Matthew, Mark, and Luke all tell us that Jesus spent forty days in the desert after his baptism in the Jordan River. "Jesus...was led by the Spirit into the desert for forty days, to be tempted by the devil" (Luke 4:1–2).

CCC 571–605, 1434–39

- Genesis 7:17–18
  Forty is the number of days the flood continued on earth. This could symbolically represent a period of cleansing, rebuilding, or atonement.

- Exodus 34:27–29
  Moses was with the Lord for forty days and nights writing the tablets of the covenant. The forty days could be a symbol of purification or preparation.

- Matthew 4:1–4
  Jesus fasts for forty days in the desert. This could be symbolic of preparation, for his death or his temptation from the Devil.

- Acts 1:1–5
  Jesus appeared to the apostles for forty days after his resurrection to speak about the kingdom of God. Here, the forty could be symbolic of a period of training or preparation of the apostles before Jesus ascends to heaven.

Living Lent

- Discuss the reflection questions as a group. Share your own list of things you prepare for and why. If participants are having a hard time answering this question, you can get them started by asking how they (or even you) prepare for these sessions.

Why Forty Days?

- Emphasize the symbolic meaning of forty days in Scripture. If you have time, go through each of the Scripture passages in the activity as a group. If not, divide participants up into four groups and assign each group one of the passages.

Lenten Symbols

- If you brought symbols to show participants, discuss those before going over the lesson text here.

- Ask participants if they've noticed other Lenten symbols around the church and what their purpose might be. (If participants don't know, use this time to explain. If there's a question about something you're not familiar with, write it down and come back with an answer next week.)

Preparing for Easter

- Remind participants of your discussion of preparation at the beginning of this session.

- Ask participants why it's important we prepare for Easter instead of just jumping into the celebration.

- Give participants time to answer the reflection questions. If you have time, ask for volunteers to share. Remind participants of the ways they've been preparing to join the Catholic Church through these sessions.

Jesus' experience in the desert reminds us of the Israelites who were freed from Egyptian slavery only to wander in the desert for forty years on their way to the Promised Land. During that time, they were tempted and they sinned. But when the devil tempted Jesus, he did not give in to temptation. Because of his faithfulness to God, Jesus overcame the temptations he faced.

In a sense, Lent is a desert experience for each of us. It's a time when we step away from the world and reflect in prayer. It's important to take time and reflect on how you're living your faith. These are the moments God's voice comes to us the clearest. Preparing for Easter during Lent by refocusing our lives on God makes us ready to take part in the Easter celebration.

Lenten Symbols

For Catholics, Lent begins with Ash Wednesday and ends before the eucharistic liturgy on Holy Thursday evening. Holy Thursday evening, Good Friday, and Holy Saturday—the sacred Triduum—are the high point of the Church's liturgical year. (See E7: *Holy Week.*) The following symbols of Lent work to bring us closer to God while preparing us for the Easter season.

Ashes: The ashes we receive on our foreheads on Ash Wednesday remind us of the passage of time and our constant need to turn away from wrongdoing. Wearing ashes on our foreheads indicates our willingness to do penance.

Purple: The color purple is a sign of reflection and conversion. The priest's vestments and Church decorations are purple during Lent.

Palms: On the Sunday before Easter, Palm Sunday, we hold palms in imitation of the people of Jerusalem who honored Jesus by throwing palm branches in his path as he rode into the city.

- Are there other Lenten symbols you've seen around your church?

- How do these symbols help prepare you for Lent?

Preparing for Easter

"The seasons and days of penance in the course of the liturgical year...are intense moments of the Church's penitential practice. These times are particularly appropriate for spiritual exercises, penitential liturgies, pilgrimages as signs of penance, voluntary self-denial such as fasting and almsgiving, and fraternal sharing."

CCC 1438

Lent focuses our attention on the reality of being human. This means our weakness and our potential to do good. Lent is also connected in a special way to the sacrament of penance. Historically, Lent was a time when people did public penance (prayers or actions that express sorrow for sin) to be reconciled with the Church. At the beginning of Lent, the bishop would place ashes on those seeking forgiveness and give them a public penance to perform. Then at Easter, they could receive the Eucharist as fully reconciled members of the Church. During Lent, many parishes still provide extra opportunities for their members to receive the sacrament of reconciliation.

- What are some ways you can prepare for Easter?

- What are some ways you've been preparing to come into the Catholic Church?

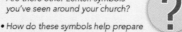

Why Is Fasting Part of Lent?

Fasting is a time-honored religious practice. (See 1 Samuel 7:5–16, 1 Kings 21:25–29, Joel 2:12–13, Acts 13:2–3, Acts 14:23.) Over the centuries, it was used as a way to concentrate better in prayer. Like other religious practices, however, fasting needs to be done in the right spirit and with an open heart.

The Church teaches that **fasting** (eating just one full meal per day) and **abstinence** (doing without certain foods) must be combined with prayer and works of charity for genuine Christian living. Fasting isn't the same as dieting, and we don't fast during Lent to lose weight or impress other people. In fact, Jesus even tells us not to call attention to ourselves when we fast (Matthew 6:16–18). Fasting is a spiritual practice that's meant to refocus attention on God.

All Catholics between the ages of fourteen and fifty-nine who are in good health are obliged to fast and abstain. In the United States, all Fridays of Lent are days of abstinence from meat. Ash Wednesday and Good Friday are days of both fasting and abstinence.

Why Should I Give Something Up?

Jesus often required his disciples to give things up so that they could follow him. Members of the early Christian community in Jerusalem gave up ownership of their goods to support the community (Acts 2:44; 4:32).

When we give something up, our goal isn't to bring suffering into our lives. It's to focus our attention on God and bring him back into the center of our lives.

This might mean turning off the television or phone for a while or postponing time with friends to have more time to spend with the Lord. Giving up time to God in prayer might be a real penance for you. Or you can use your time, talent, and treasure to serve others.

The point isn't just to give up something for Lent but to actively pay attention to our lives and how God currently fits into them. Sometimes we discover we need to give something up, other times that we need to add something.

Lent is a good time to ask:

- What do I need to feel happy?
- What occupies a lot of my time and energy? Is it using more time and energy than it should?
- Do I have unhealthy habits that push me away from God?

- *Ask yourself the questions above.*
- *How can you recenter your life on God this Lent?*

Why Is Fasting Part of Lent?

- Clarify the difference between abstinence and fasting and on which days we do which (or both) during Lent. (We abstain from meat on all Fridays during Lent as well as Ash Wednesday. We are only called to fast on Ash Wednesday and Good Fridays.)

- Discuss with participants why fasting and abstaining from certain foods is an important part of our Lenten practice.

- You could refer back to the Scripture verses Matthew 4:1–4 and Exodus 34:27–29 where both Jesus and Moses fast when in communion with God the Father.

Why Should I Give Something Up?

- If you have time, have participants answer the reflection question on their own. If you're running short on time, ask participants to complete this at home as part of their Lenten reflections.

Prayer, fasting, and almsgiving are all important parts of Lent. As a group or with a partner, brainstorm ways you can pray, fast, and give this Lent. Include how those activities can help refocus your life on God.

Prayer, fasting, and almsgiving are all important parts of Lent. As a group or with a partner, brainstorm ways you can pray, fast, and give this Lent. Include how those activities can help refocus your life on God.

Think about areas in your life where you need to make more of an effort to include God.

What could you give up or add to your life this Lent to help?

Journey of Faith for Teens: Enlightenment, E2 (826313)
Imprimi Potest: Stephen T. Rehrauer, CSsR, Provincial, Denver Province, the Redemptorists.
Imprimatur: "In accordance with CIC 827, permission to publish has been granted on June 30, 2016, by the Rev. Msgr. Mark S. Rivituso, Vicar General, Archdiocese of St. Louis. Permission to publish is an indication that nothing contrary to Church teaching is contained in this work. It does not imply any endorsement of the opinions expressed in the publication; nor is any liability assumed by this permission."
Journey of Faith for Teens © 2000, 2016 Liguori Publications, Liguori, MO 63057. All rights reserved. No part of this publication may be reproduced, distributed, stored, transmitted, or posted in any form by any means without prior written permission. To order, visit Liguori.org or call 800-325-9521. Liguori Publications, a nonprofit corporation, is an apostolate of the Redemptorists. To learn more about the Redemptorists, visit Redemptorists.com. Editors of 2016 edition: Theresa Nienaber and Pat Fosarelli, MD, DMin. Design: Lorena Mitre Jimenez. Images: Shutterstock.
Scripture texts in this work are taken from the *New American Bible*, revised edition © 2010, 1991, 1986, 1970 Confraternity of Christian Doctrine, Washington, D.C., and are used by permission of the copyright owner. All Rights Reserved. No part of the *New American Bible* may be reproduced in any form without permission in writing from the copyright owner. Excerpts from English translation of the *Catechism of the Catholic Church* for the United States of America © 1994 United States Catholic Conference, Inc. —Libreria Editrice Vaticana; English translation of the *Catechism of the Catholic Church*: Modifications from the Editio Typica © 1997 United States Catholic Conference, Inc. —Libreria Editrice Vaticana. Compliant with *The Roman Missal, Third Edition.*
Printed in the United States of America. 20 19 18 17 16 / 5 4 3 2 1. Third Edition.

Liguori
PUBLICATIONS
A Redemptorist Ministry

Journaling

Think about areas in your life where you need to make more of an effort to include God. What could you give up or add to your life this Lent to help?

Closing Prayer

Ask participants to close their eyes and reflect on what they wrote about in their journal. Then as a group, pray one decade of the Sorrowful Mysteries for this intention.

Looking Ahead

Ask participants to reflect intentionally on each day between now and the next session, thinking about ways they've honored God and ways they've fallen short. If it's helpful, they can write these reflections in their journal.

E3: Scrutinies: Looking Within

Catechism: 1434–39, 1777–94

Objectives

- Practice a daily examen of consciousness.

- Recognize that God's mercy is offered freely and to all.

- Identify the scrutinies as rites for self-searching and repentance.

Leader Meditation

Matthew 21:28–32

Ask God to forgive the times you intended to do something, but failed to follow through. Spend a moment taking a look inside yourself. What distracts you and keeps you from living your faith as fully as you intend?

Leader Preparation

- Read the lesson, this lesson plan, the Scripture passage, and the *Catechism* sections.

- Be familiar with the vocabulary terms for this lesson: conversion, scrutinies. Definitions are provided in this guide's glossary.

Welcome

Greet participants as they arrive. Check for supplies and immediate needs. Solicit questions or comments about the previous sessions and/or share new information and findings. Begin promptly.

Opening Scripture

Matthew 21:28–32

Ask a participant to light the candle and read aloud. After the reading, ask participants to spend a few moments in silence examining their hearts. When have they let others down by not following through? When have they failed to live their faith? Before beginning your discussion of the lesson handout, ask participants to think about **how we, like the second son, can change our hearts and do God's will**.

> "The education of the conscience is a lifelong task....The education of the conscience guarantees freedom and engenders peace of heart."
>
> *CCC 1784*

Journey of Faith

In Short:

- A daily examen of consciousness moves us closer to Christ.

- God's mercy is offered freely and to all.

- The scrutinies are rites for self-searching and repentance.

- *Think of a time you've regretted a choice you've made or words you've said. Why is this a regret for you?*

- *Did you try to repair the damage done? If so, why? If not, what would it take to try?*

Scrutinies: Looking Within

We all have regrets. Some of us may regret things we've said to our friends or family in a moment of anger or frustration. Others may regret letting a friendship fall apart without even trying to repair it. Others may regret letting an opportunity pass by without trying for it. Many times we regret the ways we've let ourselves down, the times we haven't acted like the people we know we really are.

As you reflect on your faith life, you may see some of these regrets in a different light. The times when we let ourselves down, the times when we hurt others, the times when we distance ourselves from God through our choices and attitudes: These regrets are our sins. And these sins can weigh on us physically, spiritually, and emotionally. The good news is that we can express sorrow for these sins, we can repair some of the hurt, we can mend our relationship with God, others, and ourselves.

The best news is that when we turn back toward God, we see that God is already turned toward us with arms outstretched.

Called to Conversion

"Jesus calls to conversion. This call is an essential part of the proclamation of the kingdom: 'The time is fulfilled, and the kingdom of God is at hand; repent, and believe in the gospel.'"

CCC 1427, citing Mark 1:15

Every trial we encounter is an opportunity to turn toward or away from God. Another word for this turning point is conversion, which comes from the Latin *convertere*, meaning "a turning, overturning, turning around; turning point; change." In spiritual terms, conversion is turning our whole self in faith and love to the God who loves us.

Some people think about conversion as simply a moral change, the decision to choose right over wrong, but conversion goes much deeper than that. Morality and law are important, but morality and law alone don't save. God saves. It's the free gift of God's love and mercy that makes true morality. When we act through God's grace, when we choose to follow God's will out of love and not fear or the desire to not get caught being bad, our conversion deepens.

CCC 1434–39; 1777–94

TEENS

Scrutinies: Looking Within

- Give participants time to answer the reflection questions on their own.

- Then ask participants, how they try to make amends for times when they haven't made the right choices. Or, how would they suggest others try to make amends.

Called to Conversion

- As a group, discuss the reflection question, *Why is just obeying the letter of the law not the same as choosing to follow the law out of love?*

Suggested responses include: Obeying the commandments to not get in trouble is different than obeying them out of faith that living this way is right; you can simply obey laws without understanding or agreeing with them; following the law out of love requires true conversion; etc....

If participants have trouble with this concept, ask them to consider the following scenario: two people donate money to charity. One does it because he or she knows charitable acts are expected of Christians, and he wants to take care of that obligation quickly. The other donates because she truly cares about the cause, and has sacrificed small things over a period of time to be able to make this donation. Which one is obeying Jesus' law to love our neighbor out of love? Why?

What Are the Scrutinies?

- Discuss the meaning of the word *scrutinize* with participants, and then ask them to connect that with the rites called the *scrutinies*.

Suggested responses include: Scrutinizing something means inspecting it very closely, that's what we're asked to do in the scrutinies; the scrutinies ask us to look for things that might remain hidden if we don't really examine our lives; etc.

First Scrutiny

- If you have time, read the full story of Jesus and the Samaritan woman out loud (John 4:5–42). Then give participants time to answer the reflection questions on their own. If you don't have time for the full story, participants can still answer the questions using only the verse, but encourage them to reflect on the whole story on their own.

- If you have time, read the full story of Jesus healing the blind man out loud (John 9:1–41). Then give participants time to answer the reflection questions on their own. If you don't have time for the full story, participants can still answer the questions using only the verse, but encourage them to reflect on the whole story on their own.

- If you have time, read aloud the full story of Jesus raising Lazarus back to life (John 11:1–45). Then give participants time to answer the reflection questions on their own. If you don't have time for the full story, participants can still answer the questions using only the verse, but encourage them to reflect on the whole story on their own.

"Our first and fundamental conversion occurs at baptism, for 'it is by faith in the Gospel and by Baptism that one renounces evil and gains salvation, that is, the forgiveness of all sins and the gift of new life.'"

CCC 1427

- *In your opinion, why is just obeying the letter of the law not the same as choosing to follow the law out of love?*

What Are the Scrutinies?

Scrutinizing something means to look at it carefully and examine it thoroughly. The rites called the **scrutinies** "are meant to uncover, then heal all that is weak, defective, or sinful in the hearts of the elect; to bring out, then strengthen all that is upright, strong, and good" (*RCIA* 141). The elect participate in three scrutinies that occur on the third, fourth, and fifth Sundays of Lent. During these scrutinies, the elect look within themselves to find anything keeping them from Christ. Then they look to Christ to heal those weaknesses and strengthen them when they face temptation. Following instruction on the mystery of sin during the catechumenate, the Church invites the elect to reflect on three Gospel stories that reveal the meaning of their upcoming baptism and the process of deepening conversion.

While baptized candidates don't participate in these scrutinies, a penitential rite, a type of scrutiny, may be offered to them on or near the second Sunday of Lent.

First Scrutiny

Christ as Living Water
In the Gospel story of Jesus meeting a Samaritan woman at a well (John 4:5–42), Jesus speaks to her of living water:

"Jesus...said to her, 'Everyone who drinks this water will be thirsty again; but whoever drinks the water I shall give will never thirst; the water I shall give will become in him a spring of water welling up to eternal life.'"

John 4:13–14

- How do Jesus' words to the Samaritan woman relate to your upcoming baptism?

- What are you hoping the living water of your baptism will refresh or make grow in you?

Second Scrutiny

Christ as the Light of the World
In the Gospel story of Jesus healing a man who was born blind (John 9:1–41), Jesus refers to himself as the Light of the World:

"'While I am in the world, I am the light of the world.' When [Jesus] had said this, he spat on the ground and made clay with the saliva, and smeared the clay on [the blind man's] eyes, and said to him, 'Go wash in the Pool of Siloam' (which means Sent). So he went and washed, and came back able to see."

John 9:5–7

- When have you been "blind," unwilling to see the light of Christ? What prevented you from seeing?

- Who or what has helped you gain new vision to recognize Christ as the light?

- What blindness (sin) do you want your upcoming baptism to wash away?

Third Scrutiny

Christ as the Resurrection and the Life
In the Gospel story of Jesus raising his friend, Lazarus, back to life (John 11:1–45), Jesus calls himself the resurrection and the life:

"Jesus said to [Martha], 'Your brother will rise.' Martha said to him, 'I know he will rise, in the resurrection on the last day.' Jesus told her, 'I am the resurrection and the life; whoever believes in me, even if he dies, will live, and everyone who lives and believes in me will never die.'"

John 11:23–26

- What does the promise of eternal life with God mean to you?

- How has your life been changing as you prepare for baptism?

- How do you expect your life to be different once you have been baptized?

Steps of the Scrutinies

1. After the homily, the elect and their godparents stand before the celebrant.

2. The assembly of the faithful prays in silence, asking that "the elect will be given a spirit of repentance, a sense of sin, and the true freedom of the children of God" (RCIA 152).

3. The celebrant (priest or deacon) invites the elect to pray in silence and may suggest they bow their heads or kneel as "a sign of their inner spirit of repentance" (RCIA 152).

4. The celebrant offers prayers of intercession for the elect.

5. The celebrant offers a prayer that the elect be "freed from the effects of sin and from the influence of the devil" (RCIA 144).

6. The celebrant may lay hands on the head of each of the elect.

7. The celebrant makes a final prayer for all the elect with his hands outstretched over them.

8. The celebrant either dismisses them to reflect on the Scripture readings or invites them to return to their seats for the Liturgy of the Eucharist.

"The scrutinies are celebrated in order to deliver the elect from the power of sin and Satan, to protect them from temptation, and to give them strength in Christ, who is the way, the truth, and the life. These rites, therefore, should…deepen their resolve to hold fast to Christ and to carry out their decision to love God above all."

RCIA 141

Praying the Examen

Saint Ignatius of Loyola (1491–1556) was very practical when it came to prayer. He even created an outline for the daily examination of our lives which he encouraged his brothers to use as a way of growing towards and better serving the Lord. Saint Ignatius taught that the foundation to a healthy spirituality required two things: finding God in all things and constantly working to gain the freedom to cooperate with God's will.

This daily exercise, called the Examen (or Examen of Consciousness), has been—and still is—used by many Christians. It is a simple prayer for people who are continually seeking to do the Lord's will.

There are six simple steps to the Examen, and they only take about fifteen minutes to complete:

1. *Recall you are in the presence of God.* Through prayer, we place ourselves in God's presence in an especially attentive way. Ask the Holy Spirit to help you look at your life with love.

2. *Look at your day with gratitude.* Remember each detail and event of your day with gratitude. Every single event is God's gift. Take care to notice what you received and what you gave back. Thank God for everything.

3. *Ask the Holy Spirit for help.* Ask the Holy Spirit to come into your heart and help you look at your actions clearly. Ask for help with understanding your limitations.

4. *Review your day.* Pay attention to the details, the context of what happened, and your actions. As you review, notice your interior motives and feelings: *When did you fail? When did you love? What patterns and habits do you see? Where did you see signs of God's grace?*

5. *Reconcile and resolve.* Talk with Jesus about what you did and didn't do. If you failed to love in some way, tell Jesus you're sorry and ask him to be with you the next time a similar situation arises. Give praise for the good things and thank the Lord for being with you when you avoided a wrong choice or resisted temptation. Feel sorrow when you apologize but also feel the gratitude when you give thanks for God's work inside your heart.

6. End the Examen by praying the Our Father.

Praying the Examen

- Set aside fifteen minutes to guide participants through praying the Examen. Encourage participants to use their journal to write down their reflection if it's helpful (they will not be asked to share).

- Have participants transition from the Examen to their journal prompt for this session.

There is no situation so desperate it is beyond the grace of God. When we accept God's grace we can be fully restored, but this restoration is a process, and we will continue to grow and struggle in life. Imagine this process in your mind. Are there different stages of restoration? Will there be ups and downs? How will God be at work? On your own or with a partner, describe this process of restoration in writing, as a visual, or in some other way.

There is no situation so desperate that it is beyond the grace of God. When we accept God's grace we can be fully restored, but this restoration is a process, and we will continue to grow and to struggle in life. Imagine this process in your mind. Are there different stages of restoration? Will there be ups and downs? How will God be at work? On your own or with a partner, describe this process of restoration in writing, as a visual, or in some other way.

After reflecting on the Examen, are there any events of your day or choices you made that really stand out to you? This can be a time you clearly saw God at work or a time you struggled. Spend time reflecting on that moment in writing.

Journey of Faith for Teens: Enlightenment, E3 (826313)
Imprimi Potest: Stephen T. Rehrauer, CSsR, Provincial, Denver Province, the Redemptorists.
Imprimatur: "In accordance with CIC 827, permission to publish has been granted on June 30, 2016, by the Rev. Msgr. Mark S. Rivituso, Vicar General, Archdiocese of St. Louis. Permission to publish is an indication that nothing contrary to Church teaching is contained in this work. It does not imply any endorsement of the opinions expressed in the publication, nor is any liability assumed by this permission."
Journey of Faith for Teens © 2000, 2016 Liguori Publications, Liguori, MO 63057. All rights reserved. No part of this publication may be reproduced, distributed, stored, transmitted, or posted in any form by any means without prior written permission. To order, visit Liguori.org or call 800-325-9521. Liguori Publications, a nonprofit corporation, is an apostolate of the Redemptorists. To learn more about the Redemptorists, visit Redemptorists.com. Contributing Writer: Fr. James P. Dunning, PhD. The Examen is taken from the *Catholic Update* "Examen of Consciousness" by Phyllis Zagano. Editors of 2016 edition: Theresa Nienaber and Pat Fosarelli, MD, DMin. Design: Lorena Mitre Jimenez. Images: Shutterstock.
Scripture texts in this work are taken from the *New American Bible*, revised edition © 2010, 1991, 1986, 1970 Confraternity of Christian Doctrine, Washington, D.C., and are used by permission of the copyright owner. All Rights Reserved. No part of the *New American Bible* may be reproduced in any form without permission in writing from the copyright owner. Excerpts from English translation of the *Catechism of the Catholic Church* for the United States of America © 1994 United States Catholic Conference, Inc.—Libreria Editrice Vaticana. English translation of the *Catechism of the Catholic Church: Modifications from the Editio Typica* © 1997 United States Catholic Conference, Inc.—Libreria Editrice Vaticana. Excerpts from *The Rites of the Catholic Church, Volume One* (abbreviated *RCIA* herein) © 1990 Liturgical Press. Compliant with *The Roman Missal, Third Edition.* Printed in the United States of America. 20 19 18 17 16 / 5 4 3 2 1. Third Edition.

Liguori
PUBLICATIONS
A Redemptorist Ministry

Journaling

After reflecting on the Examen, are there any events of your day or choices you made that really stand out to you? This can be a time you clearly saw God at work or a time you struggled. Spend time reflecting on that moment in writing.

Closing Prayer

Close this lesson by inviting the class to offer their petitions and by praying this abbreviated litany.

L: Lord have mercy.

R: Lord have mercy.

L: Christ, have mercy.

R: Christ have mercy.

L: Lord, hear us.

R: Lord, graciously hear us.

L: Lord, guide us as we make our own sincere evaluation of conscience. Send your Holy Spirit to guide us. Help us to feel the touch of our Father's love. You who are love itself, have mercy on us and all our spoken and unspoken petitions.

Looking Ahead

As participants prepare for the next session, ask them to reflect on how their beliefs have changed as they've come to know the Catholic Church and to reflect on what they currently believe.

E4: The Creed

Catechism: 166–175, 185–197

Objectives

- Recognize the deep meaning of each major phase or statement in the Nicene Creed.

- Describe in their own words the origin of the Creed.

- Explain why the Creed is necessary for Church unity.

Leader Meditation

The Nicene Creed

Read over the Nicene Creed, reflecting on the truth expressed in each phrase. Prepare to share your reflections and these truths as you discuss this lesson.

Leader Preparation

- Read the lesson, this lesson plan, the Scripture passage, and the *Catechism* sections.

- Be familiar with the vocabulary terms for this lesson: creed, begotten, consubstantial, catholic, apostolic. Definitions are provided in this guide's glossary.

Welcome

Greet participants as they arrive. Check for supplies and immediate needs. Solicit questions or comments about the previous sessions and/or share new information and findings. Begin promptly.

Opening Scripture

Romans 10:9–11

Ask a volunteer to light the candle and read aloud. Explain that every time we say the Creed at Mass, we are declaring our belief in the Trinity, the paschal mystery, and everything that stems from them. Read the Nicene Creed aloud. Before beginning your discussion of the lesson handout, ask participants to think about **why it's important for us to confess our beliefs out loud**.

> "To say the Credo with faith is to enter into communion with God...and also with the whole Church which transmits the faith to us and in whose midst we believe."
>
> CCC 197

Journey of Faith

In Short:

- The Creed is rooted in the early Church.
- The Creed summarizes major principles of faith.
- The Creed unifies us as a Church.

Think of one club, team, or organization to which you presently belong.

- *What is the purpose of this group?*
- *What beliefs help all its members work toward a common goal?*

The Creed

The word **creed** comes from a word that means "I believe." The Church's need for an established set of truths developed in the first centuries after Christ when Christians began asking difficult questions about the nature of God. People needed answers to questions not addressed in the New Testament record of Jesus' teachings. These questions might be similar to those you have about God today.

- How can one God be three persons—Father, Son, and Holy Spirit?
- How can Jesus be both God and human?
- What is God's kingdom like?

The Nicene Creed was the Church's first attempt to establish a set of beliefs for all Christians.

Just as any organization has written purposes, goals, and requirements to help members understand what the organization is all about, the Church needs an official statement of beliefs for its members—our Creed.

Let's take a closer look at the beliefs of the Catholic Church.

I believe in one God, the Father almighty...

We live in a technical, scientific world where nearly everything can be fully explained or proven. This is what makes faith so difficult. We make the decision to believe in something that can't be easily explained or proven. Because we're human, we think about God in human terms. Unfortunately, this sometimes limits God to our own experience. But God is so much more. Perhaps the most difficult step of the faith journey is being OK with not completely understanding the nature of God because it goes so far beyond human experience.

Even the prophets of the Old Testament were limited to describing God in human terms. But there's still a lot we can learn about God from our humanity. After all, we were created in God's image and likeness, and God did become man.

Read Isaiah 49:15–16.

- *What is the prophet attempting to tell us about God?*

CCC 166–175, 185–197

I believe in one God, the Father almighty...

- Read Isaiah 49:15–16 as a group. Ask participants to answer the question on their own or with a partner, "What is the prophet attempting to tell us about God?"

- *Responses include: God loves us like a mother loves her infant, God will always have tenderness toward his children, God won't forget us like an earthly parent might, God has written us into his being.*

The Creed

- Ask participants to recall why the Church needed to develop the Creed. Using the list on page 1 of the handout as your guide, list as a class other faith questions people might have that are answered by the Creed.

Suggested responses include: Who created the world and universe; why did Jesus have to die; will Jesus come again; etc.

- Give participants time to respond to the question in the introduction. Ask participants to share why it's important for a group working toward a common goal to establish their beliefs in a "creed."

Suggested responses include: the Constitution, the Pledge of Allegiance, and corporate mission statements.

- Emphasize that the Creed is a communal statement of our Catholic beliefs, it isn't just about our personal beliefs, relationships, or practices.

I believe in one Lord Jesus Christ, the Only Begotten Son of God...

- Read John 13:3–17 as a group. Ask participants to answer the question on their own or with a partner, "What does this passage tell us about Jesus and therefore about God?"

Responses include: Jesus is our teacher and master, Jesus came to serve, Jesus calls us to serve others as well, Jesus as man is our model for moral living.

And by the Holy Spirit was incarnate of the Virgin Mary, and became man...

- Ask participants to explain in their own words what it means for Jesus to be *consubstantial* with the Father and *incarnate* of Mary.

I believe in one Lord Jesus Christ, the Only Begotten Son of God...

The best way to understand God is to carefully study the words and actions of Jesus. Jesus is God in human form. The more we learn about Jesus, the better we understand God. The New Testament gives us important information about the person Jesus.

> Refer to John 13:3–17.
> - What does this passage tell us about Jesus and therefore about God?

Begotten, not made, consubstantial with the Father...

Here we are faced with the mystery of the Trinity. The word **begotten** means that Jesus and God are of the same nature. **Consubstantial** means Jesus is one in being with the Father. Human beings can only make things that are separate from themselves. This statement expresses the Catholic belief that Jesus is God, "true God from true God."

For us men and for our salvation he came down from heaven...

God loves us so much that God came to dwell among all human beings (which is what is meant by "men") in the person Jesus. Through Jesus, we know God and are shown the way to eternal life with God.

And by the Holy Spirit was incarnate of the Virgin Mary, and became man...

Through the Holy Spirit, Mary became pregnant—a true miracle. Jesus was given a human body and made flesh but is both fully God and fully human. As he grew, Jesus experienced all the joys, sorrows, difficulties, and even doubts that are a part of human life.

> - Reflect on what you've read so far. In your own words, explain what it means for Jesus to be consubstantial with the Father and incarnate of Mary.

For our sake he was crucified under Pontius Pilate...

Jesus' perfect love was a threat to the sinful side of human nature. Evil often lashes out against goodness. Jesus died a terrible death because of humankind's sinfulness.

And rose again on the third day...

The resurrection of Jesus is central to our Catholic faith. Jesus is the Light of the World. We celebrate his triumph over darkness at the Easter Vigil on Holy Saturday night and on Easter, the greatest celebration of the Church year.

Following the resurrection, Jesus' human body became a glorified body—one not subject to normal physical limitations and death. Some of his closest friends did not recognize him—until his actions revealed who he was.

He ascended into heaven and is seated at the right hand of the Father.

The ascension does not mean that Jesus is far away from us in a distant heaven. Quite the opposite is true. Being at the right hand of God means that Jesus fully shares God's desires for creation and is with all his people at all times as Savior and Lord. Jesus speaks to us in the Bible, touches us in the sacraments and in the love we share with one another, and is with us when we gather in his name.

He will come again in glory to judge the living and the dead and his kingdom will have no end.

Christ alone is our final judge. His kingdom is a family of love that unites the saints of heaven with God's people here on earth. Our Church calls this the communion of saints. Heaven is not limited by time or space.

I believe in the Holy Spirit, the Lord, the giver of life...

The Catholic Church holds that the Holy Spirit is the third person of the Trinity and is the perfect love eternally coming from the Father and the Son. We find the Holy Spirit in all that is good, true, and honorable in creation and in ourselves. The Spirit is the sacred power that influences us to act in kindness and love.

The following is the Profession of Faith that Catholics make nearly every Sunday at Mass (sometimes the Apostles' Creed is used). It is also called the Nicene Creed because it was adopted as the true belief of the early Church by a council of bishops meeting in the city of Nicaea in the year 325. Carefully read the following:

The Nicene Creed

I believe in one God,
the Father almighty,
maker of heaven and earth,
of all things visible and invisible.

I believe in one Lord Jesus Christ,
the Only Begotten Son of God,
born of the Father before all ages.
God from God, Light from Light,
true God from true God,
begotten, not made, consubstantial with the Father;
through him all things were made.
For us men and for our salvation
he came down from heaven,
and by the Holy Spirit was incarnate of the Virgin Mary,
and became man.
For our sake he was crucified under Pontius Pilate,
he suffered death and was buried,
and rose again on the third day
in accordance with the Scriptures.
He ascended into heaven
and is seated at the right hand of the Father.
He will come again in glory
to judge the living and the dead
and his kingdom will have no end.

I believe in the Holy Spirit, the Lord, the giver of life,
who proceeds from the Father and the Son,
who with the Father and the Son is adored and glorified,
who has spoken through the prophets.

I believe in one, holy, catholic and apostolic Church.
I confess one Baptism for the forgiveness of sins
and I look forward to the resurrection of the dead
and the life of the world to come. Amen.

I believe in one, holy, catholic and apostolic Church.

Here, the word **catholic** means "universal" or "whole." This acknowledges Christ's desire that all his followers be united in him. The term **apostolic** means that the Church's authority and teachings are rooted in the apostles, whom Jesus commissioned to preach. We, too, are apostles of Christ, sent to bring his light to the world.

I confess one Baptism for the forgiveness of sins...

At baptism, we become full members of Christ's Church. Baptism removes the power that sin had over us, strengthens us with grace, and fills us with the Holy Spirit.

I look forward to the resurrection of the dead and the life of the world to come.

Eternal life with God in heaven brings us knowledge and love that cannot be fully experienced here on earth or fully expressed in words we could understand.

The Catholic Church also acknowledges the reality of hell, a state of eternal separation from God that some people choose. The Church believes that for those who will die with imperfections that keep them from being one with God, God's loving mercy and his forgiveness allow for a temporary state of purification called purgatory. After death, those who die in God's grace and friendship find God's loving mercy and forgiveness in this temporary state of purification. Purgatory may be described as an experience of God's healing following death that allows us to enter into perfect union with God.

• Reflect on what you've read so far. If baptism removes the power sin has over us, why do we need purgatory?

Amen.

This means, "So be it." In other words, "Let this all come to pass." When we end the Creed with "Amen," we affirm that everything we've professed is true.

I confess one Baptism for the forgiveness of sins...

• Remind participants this includes baptism into other Christian communities. This is why already-baptized candidates are not rebaptized at the Easter Vigil.

I look forward to the resurrection of the dead and the life of the world to come.

• Pause for participants to reflect on what they've read so far. Encourage them to write any questions or insights into their journal and give them the opportunity to ask questions. If there are question you can't answer, make note of them and seek out answers for the next session.

• Discuss as a group, "If baptism removes the power sin has over us, why do we need purgatory?"

Suggested responses include: Our original sin is forgiven at baptism, but we can still sin after we've been baptized—that's why we have reconciliation. Purgatory gives us the chance to be made ready for heaven because even after baptism we aren't perfect.

As a class or with a partner, pick two to three sections of the Nicene Creed that you found confusing and summarize them in your own words. Share your summaries with the class.

As a class or with a partner, pick two to three sections of the Nicene Creed that you find confusing and summarize them in your own words. Share your summaries with the class.

Why is it important for all Catholics to profess and believe the same thing? Describe another example of when it's important for all members of a group to share common beliefs.

Journey of Faith for Teens: Enlightenment, E4 (826313)
Imprimi Potest: Stephen T. Rehrauer, CSsR, Provincial, Denver Province, the Redemptorists
Imprimatur: "In accordance with CIC 827, permission to publish has been granted on June 30, 2016, by the Rev. Msgr. Mark S. Rivituso, Vicar General, Archdiocese of St. Louis. Permission to publish is an indication that nothing contrary to Church teaching is contained in this work. It does not imply any endorsement of the opinions expressed in the publication; nor is any liability assumed by this permission."
Journey of Faith for Teens © 2000, 2016 Liguori Publications, Liguori, MO 63057. All rights reserved. No part of this publication may be reproduced, distributed, stored, transmitted, or posted in any form by any means without prior written permission. To order, visit Liguori.org or call 800-325-9521. Liguori Publications, a nonprofit corporation, is an apostolate of the Redemptorists. To learn more about the Redemptorists, visit Redemptorists.com. Editors of 2016 edition: Theresa Nienaber and Pat Fosarelli, MD, DMin. Design: Lorena Mitre Jimenez. Images: Shutterstock.
Scripture texts in this work are taken from the *New American Bible*, revised edition © 2010, 1991, 1986, 1970 Confraternity of Christian Doctrine, Washington, D.C., and are used by permission of the copyright owner. All Rights Reserved. No part of the *New American Bible* may be reproduced in any form without permission in writing from the copyright owner. Excerpts from English translation of the *Catechism of the Catholic Church for the United States of America* © 1994 United States Catholic Conference, Inc.—*Libreria Editrice Vaticana;* English translation of the *Catechism of the Catholic Church: Modifications from the Editio Typica* © 1997 United States Catholic Conference, Inc.—*Libreria Editrice Vaticana.* Compliant with *The Roman Missal, Third Edition.*
Printed in the United States of America. 20 19 18 17 16 / 5 4 3 2 1. Third Edition.

Liguori
PUBLICATIONS
A Redemptorist Ministry

Journaling

Why is it important for all Catholics to profess and believe the same thing? Describe another example of when it's important for all members of a group to share common beliefs.

Closing Prayer

Ask participants to voice any special intentions for this week. Mention the First Scrutiny (third Sunday). You may want to close with a prayer they will hear in the Presentation. Recite a Glory Be together.

Looking Ahead

The core message of our faith—and the Creed—is that Christ suffered, died, and rose again so that we could have eternal life. Before next class, read a passion account from one of the Gospels, taking note of the steps and events along Christ's path.

E5: The Way of the Cross

Catechism: 2663–2669

Objectives

- Recall the historical roots of the Way of the Cross and its significance as a tradition and prayer form.

- Reflect on the traditional fourteen stations, examining their foundation in the Gospels.

- Recognize that following Jesus requires us to carry our own crosses.

Leader Meditation

Matthew 26—27; Mark 14—15; Luke 22—23; or John 18:12—19:38

Slowly and reflectively read any one of the passion accounts. Allow yourself to become a part of the crowd, a witness to all that is happening. Remember that Jesus Christ submitted to his passion and death to open the gates of eternal life so we might come to know and share the abundant life of Christ.

Leader Preparation

- Read the lesson, this lesson plan, the Scripture passage, and the *Catechism* sections.

- Organize to have this lesson taught in church so that the group can move from station to station throughout the lesson. If this isn't possible, try to have images prepared for use in your regular room or encourage participants to walk through the stations at some time during the next few days.

Welcome

Greet participants as they arrive. Check for supplies and immediate needs. Solicit questions or comments about the previous sessions and/or share new information and findings. Begin promptly.

Opening Scripture

Mark 15:21–39

Ask a participant to light the candle and read aloud. Ask participants to empathize with the emotions of Jesus' grieving mother and his beloved friends. Before beginning your discussion of the lesson handout, ask participants to think about **being witnesses to the suffering and death of Jesus. What would their thoughts and feelings be?**

> "Christian prayer loves to follow the way of the cross in the Savior's steps. The stations from the Praetorium to Golgotha and the tomb trace the way of Jesus, who by his holy Cross has redeemed the world."
>
> CCC 2669

Journey of Faith

In Short:

- The Way of the Cross has roots in the early Church.
- The traditional fourteen stations mark the path of Jesus' passion and death.
- Following Jesus requires us to carry our own crosses.

The Way of the Cross

Ron was starting his sophomore year with the same group of friends he'd had forever. Normally they'd just hang out at school, go to soccer practice, and then go to someone's house. Their parents always knew where they were and that they were having fun.

But now it seemed like there was just one thing Ron's friends liked to do—get drunk. Ron was lying to his parents, forgetting homework assignments, skipping practice. And he was miserable.

He needed new friends. Ron knew that's what he had to do. But doing the right thing meant losing the friends he'd always had. It also meant starting over and the possibility of being all alone.

- What would you advise Ron to do?
- What would you do in a similar situation?

"Whoever wishes to come after me must deny himself, take up his cross, and follow me."

Matthew 16:24

Following Jesus involves more than being kind or going to Mass every week. To follow Jesus, we must follow his way of the cross.

A prayer that helps us understand what this means is the Way (or Stations) of the Cross. Fourteen scenes (or crosses) help us reflect on and follow in the steps Jesus took on his way to his death.

The Way of the Cross reminds us of Jesus' suffering and reminds us that we are not alone in our own suffering. Being called to live and love like Christ means we will have our own crosses to bear. The Way of the Cross reminds us that by carrying these crosses we are following in the footsteps of Christ.

"Christian prayer loves to follow the way of the cross in the Savior's steps. The stations... trace the way of Jesus, who by his holy Cross has redeemed the world."

CCC 2669

I. Jesus Is Condemned to Death

"[The crowd] only shouted the louder, 'Crucify him.' So Pilate...released Barabbas to them and, after he had Jesus scourged, handed him over to be crucified."

Mark 15:14–15

TEENS

CCC 2663–2669

The Way of the Cross

- Discuss the reflection questions as a group.

- Ask participants if they've ever felt worried or afraid of doing the right thing. Discuss why doing the right thing can sometimes be a difficult choice.

- Before you start the Way of the Cross, ask participants what they think it means to really follow Jesus.

Suggested responses include: Choosing the right thing even though it's difficult, serving and sacrificing for others, seeking forgiveness when we do wrong, etc.

- Pray the Way of the Cross with the group. Have willing participants take turns reading the prayers from the lesson that accompany each station. Pause at each station to allow students an opportunity to write in their prayer journal or to reflect in silence.

- Encourage questions as well (this is still your instructional session). It's OK to spend more time at a station where participants have more questions or that starts an on-topic discussion.

Jesus, you faced those who judged and condemned you, but you did not hate. You struggled with fear and humiliation, yet you continued your mission. *How often do I judge others instead of looking at myself? How often do I stay quiet when I should speak up?*

Jesus, teach us to tolerate criticism and ridicule when we stand up for what is right. Give us the courage to continue our mission.

II. Jesus Bears His Cross

"Carrying the cross himself he went out to what is called the Place of the Skull."

John 19:17

Jesus, when you took the cross upon your shoulders, you did it willingly. You showed us your true power. You trusted the will of your Father. You continued on, despite your tremendous burden. *How often do I give up in my daily struggles? When have I been afraid to trust God's plan?*

Through your Holy Spirit, strengthen us so that we carry our daily crosses without complaining or losing heart. When we feel ready to give up, teach us to turn to you for encouragement and understanding. Open our eyes so we may see you in the faces of those who care for us.

III. Jesus Falls the First Time

Jesus, the burden of the cross caused the blood to flow from your wounds and the strength to flow from your body. You fell to the dust, but you pulled yourself up. Exhausted and suffering, you shouldered your cross; you continued to struggle forward. *When have I tried to find an excuse to give up my cross or pass it off to someone else?*

Teach us to stand back up when we fall, when we get off the right track, when we fail to follow your footsteps. When we land in the dust, guide us back to you. Keep us away from the false gods that will tempt us with comfort and ease. Show us how to forgive ourselves and to cling to our faith and our hope in you.

IV. Jesus Meets His Mother

Jesus, you experienced your mother's indescribable pain as she looked at you in your anguish. You gazed with compassion on her ravaged face. You understood that there is no greater human suffering than the pain of a parent losing a child. *How have my parents supported me carrying my crosses?*

Teach us to cherish those we love. Remind us never to take them for granted. Instill in us the courage to show our love and express our feelings. Give us hearts that are grateful for the chance to share our lives with loving friends and family.

V. Jesus Is Helped by Simon

"They pressed into service a passer-by, Simon, a Cyrenian...to carry his cross."

Mark 15:21

Jesus, you shared your burden with Simon, showing that we all need help at times. *When have I offered to help share another's burden?*

Often we are asked to help or to serve, but we refuse. Sometimes we are offered help, but we choose not to accept. Help us to appreciate that all who positively touch our lives are part of your plan.

VI. Veronica Wipes the Face of Jesus

Jesus, what great courage it must have taken for Veronica to defy the soldiers and offer you comfort! *When have I gone against the popular to do the right?*

What we do for others, we do for you. When we have the courage to comfort someone or welcome a lonely classmate into our circle of friends, we are offering you comfort and friendship. Give us vision and wisdom, that we may find you in the face of every person we meet.

VII. Jesus Falls a Second Time

Climbing with your heavy burden, Lord, your body gave out once more. You showed us that it's all right to fail sometimes. *Do I handle my failures with grace and courage?*

Teach us to look with understanding upon the failings of others. May we be slow to criticize and judge but quick to offer our help!

VIII. Jesus Speaks to the Women

"Jesus turned to [the women] and said, 'Daughters of Jerusalem, do not weep for me; weep instead for yourselves and for your children.'"

Luke 23:28

Lord, it is the women who are deeply saddened by your suffering. But you told them to weep for their own oppression. *How do I look at those who have less than me?*

Teach us to look with compassion upon the suffering of those around us, especially those without status or power. Help us to act justly and become more aware of the injustice that surrounds us.

IX. Jesus Falls a Third Time

Jesus, the burden of your cross overpowered you once more. With your last ounce of strength, you pulled yourself up. *Do I use my courage to get up again and again when I fall? How often do I blame God for sending tragedy into my life?*

Lord, you give us hope, yet we too often choose despair. Teach us to be a people of hope even when the weight of our crosses seems unbearable.

X. Jesus Is Stripped of His Garments

"They took his clothes and divided them into four shares, a share for each soldier."

John 19:23

Jesus, you suffered through the humiliation of being stripped of your clothes. Yet, you did not hate those who humiliated you. *How do I respond when humiliated?*

Teach us not to lash out at or seek to get even with those who hurt us. Give us the courage and the wisdom to forgive—again and again.

XI. Jesus Is Nailed to the Cross

"There they crucified him, and with him two others, one on either side, with Jesus in the middle."

John 19:18

Jesus, with each blow of the hammer, the burning metal penetrated your flesh. You endured that agony for love. *What am I willing to suffer for the love of God?*

Loving Christ, help us not to crucify others by cruel words or unkind actions. Teach us to act and react lovingly, to build up your body instead of tearing it apart.

XII. Jesus Dies on the Cross

"Jesus cried out in a loud voice, 'Father, into your hands I commend my spirit'; and...he breathed his last."

Luke 23:46

Before the activity, tell students that, historically, the number of stations varied but eventually fourteen became the norm. The addition of the fifteenth station is fairly recent and this additional station is not always prayed.

Some people pray a fifteenth station, the Resurrection of Christ. Write a brief prayer or reflection to use if you were going to pray this station.

Jesus, you showed us how to give life and love through the ultimate sacrifice. *What does this mean for me?*

You gave everything for us, but sometimes we withhold things from you. Help us to understand that by your death you show us how to die and rise each day.

XIII. Jesus Is Taken From the Cross

"[Joseph] came from the Jewish town of Arimathea and was awaiting the kingdom of God. He went to Pilate and asked for the body of Jesus."

Luke 23:51–52

Jesus, you taught us to trust in you even when everything seemed hopeless. Those at the foot of your cross remained, even though they were shaken. *Do I remember to hope in you even when I'm shaken?*

Loving Christ, often we are weak in our faith as we see suffering and death in the world. Teach us that from loss and grief can come growth and redemption. Help us to bring light to the dark places in our world.

XIV. Jesus Is Buried in the Tomb

"After [Joseph] had taken [Jesus'] body down, he wrapped it in a linen cloth and laid him in a rock-hewn tomb."

Luke 23:53

Jesus, since it was almost time for the Passover, your broken body was hurriedly wrapped in a shroud, rushed to the tomb, and left on a stone slab. Obeying the Jewish law, no one took time to clean and anoint your body. *Do I take the time to remember the oppressed and forgotten?*

Lord, teach us to remember that death cannot destroy real love. Nor can it destroy faith or hope. These things are much greater than death.

Some people pray a fifteenth station, the Resurrection of Christ. Write a brief prayer or reflection to use if you were going to pray this station.

Which of the stations today was the most difficult for you to respond to? Why?

Journey of Faith for Teens: Enlightenment, E5 (826313)
Imprimi Potest: Stephen T. Rehrauer, CSsR, Provincial, Denver Province, the Redemptorists.
Imprimatur: "In accordance with CIC 827, permission to publish has been granted on June 30, 2016, by the Rev. Msgr. Mark S. Rivituso, Vicar General, Archdiocese of St. Louis. Permission to publish is an indication that nothing contrary to Church teaching is contained in this work. It does not imply any endorsement of the opinions expressed in the publication, nor is any liability assumed by this permission."
Journey of Faith for Teens © 2000, 2016 Liguori Publications, Liguori, MO 63057. All rights reserved. No part of this publication may be reproduced, distributed, stored, transmitted, or posted in any form by any means without prior written permission. To order, visit Liguori.org or call 800-325-9521. Liguori Publications, a nonprofit corporation, is an apostolate of the Redemptorists. To learn more about the Redemptorists, visit Redemptorists.com. Editors of 2016 edition: Theresa Nienaber and Pat Fosarelli, MD, DMin. Design: Lorena Mitre Jimenez. Images: Shutterstock.
Scripture texts in this work are taken from the *New American Bible*, revised edition © 2010, 1991, 1986, 1970 Confraternity of Christian Doctrine, Washington, D.C., and are used by permission of the copyright owner. All Rights Reserved. No part of the *New American Bible* may be reproduced in any form without permission in writing from the copyright owner. Excerpts from English translation of the *Catechism of the Catholic Church* for the United States of America © 1994 United States Catholic Conference, Inc.—Libreria Editrice Vaticana; English translation of the *Catechism of the Catholic Church: Modifications from the Editio Typica* © 1997 United States Catholic Conference, Inc.—Libreria Editrice Vaticana. Compliant with *The Roman Missal, Third Edition.*
Printed in the United States of America. 20 19 18 17 16 / 5 4 3 2 1. Third Edition.

Liguori
PUBLICATIONS
A Redemptorist Ministry

Journaling

Which of the stations today was the most difficult for you to respond to? Why?

Closing Prayer

As a group, pray the following reflection on the resurrection of Christ:

Jesus, you fulfilled your promise and rose from the dead on the third day. The gift of your death and resurrection makes it possible for us to die and rise. You make it possible for us to become whole and to transform the world. We praise you for the gift of life. Amen.

Looking Ahead

Jesus doesn't ask us to follow him on our own strength. He gives us grace through the sacraments and traditions of our faith. Before the next session, ask participants to think about the ways, prayers, and sacraments Jesus gives us to encourage us as we carry our own crosses.

E6: The Lord's Prayer

Catechism: 2759–2772

Objectives

- Recognize that Jesus invites us to call God our Father.

- Reflect on each of the seven petitions contained in the Lord's Prayer.

- Recall that the Lord's Prayer was the prayer given by Jesus to his disciples.

Leader Meditation

Matthew 6:5–15

Examine your experiences with prayer. Is it a spontaneous part of your daily life? Do you believe God listens to you? How well do you accept God's response when prayers aren't answered according to *your* will? Are you able to hear and see the loving response of God, even when you are feeling disappointed?

Leader Preparation

- Read the lesson, this lesson plan, the Scripture passage, and the *Catechism* sections.

Welcome

Greet participants as they arrive. Check for supplies and immediate needs. Solicit questions or comments about the previous sessions and/or share new information and findings. Begin promptly.

Opening Scripture

Matthew 6:5–15

Ask a participant to light the candle and read aloud. After the reading, encourage discussion about prayer and God's response. Assure participants that sometimes prayers we think have gone unanswered have still been heard by God. Sometimes God's answers are beyond our understanding. As you begin discussion of the lesson handout, ask participants to think about **how God answers their prayers and how they feel about their personal prayer life.**

> "When Jesus prays he is already teaching us how to pray. His prayer to his Father is the theological path (the path of faith, hope, and charity) of our prayer to God."
>
> *CCC 2607*

Journey of Faith

In Short:

- Jesus invites us to call God our Father.
- Jesus taught his disciples the Lord's Prayer.
- The Lord's Prayer contains seven petitions.

The Lord's Prayer

> *Our Father, who art in heaven,*
> *hallowed be thy name;*
> *thy kingdom come;*
> *thy will be done on earth as it is in heaven.*
> *Give us this day our daily bread;*
> *and forgive us our trespasses*
> *as; we forgive those who trespass against us;*
> *and lead us not into temptation,*
> *but deliver us from evil.*
> *Amen.*

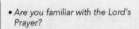

- Are you familiar with the Lord's Prayer?
- If yes, what does it mean to you? If not, what's your first impression?

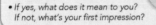

Jesus' Advice on Prayer

In the Gospels, Jesus gives us some pretty specific instructions on how to pray. According to Jesus' teaching, the most important issue is our attitude. We should pray because we want to develop a closer, personal relationship with God.

It was common practice for the devout Jews of Jesus' time to pray in public at set times. Routine and community can be great motivators in our prayer life, but Jesus encourages us to be aware of our interior motives. Our goal shouldn't be to "get caught" praying so others are impressed by our piousness. Jesus tells us:

> "When you pray, do not be like the hypocrites, who love to stand and pray in the synagogues and on street corners so that others may see them. Amen, I say to you, they have received their reward. But when you pray, go to your inner room, close the door, and pray to your Father in secret. And your Father who sees in secret will repay you."
>
> *Matthew 6:5–6*

When "one of [Jesus'] disciples said to him, 'Lord, teach us to pray'" (Luke 11:1), Jesus responded by sharing the Lord's Prayer.

CCC 2759–72

The Lord's Prayer

- Discuss the reflection questions as a group, and then ask participants to discuss their different images of a "father" or parent. Be sensitive to any participant who may have a difficult or nonexistent relationship with his or her father, and encourage participants to think not only of their biological parents but of any adult who genuinely cares about them.

Our Father, who art in heaven...

- Engage in Ignatian prayer (imaginative prayer) using the prayer suggestion. While the focus of this lesson should be on the words to the Lord's Prayer itself, these prayer suggestions are included to keep participants engaged, as well as actively connecting each line of the prayer to their own lives.

- Give participants time to answer the reflection question on their own. Ask for volunteers to share, or share your own response to this prompt.

Hallowed be thy name; thy kingdom come...

- Ask participants what they think "hallowed" means in this context. If they struggle with this definition, let them know it means "holy" and that this line is saying that "Our Father in heaven's" name is and should be kept "holy."

- As a group, discuss the questions, *How do you see other people in your community building the kingdom of God? Your country? The world?* Ask participants why they think it's important for us to build the kingdom of God on earth and not just wait for heaven.

Suggested responses include: Evangelizing others to spread the good news, protesting actions that don't support or promote life, sharing and serving others, etc. Using Jesus as our model we see how to live on earth, being a Christian means working toward the kingdom of God in life, building the kingdom of God on earth helps more people learn what it means to follow God, etc.

In the words Jesus taught us, we pray:

Our Father, who art in heaven...

Jesus called God *Abba*, a personal name given by children to their father (like daddy). To call God by this intimate name was unheard of in Jewish custom. By inviting his disciples, and us, to call God *Abba* Jesus invites us into a close, personal relationship with God and reminds us that we are God's beloved children.

It can be challenging to see God as our daddy, as the perfect parent. Especially if we have a difficult or strained relationship with our own parents. That's OK. As humans, even our parents make mistakes. As you build this image of God as father, draw upon the positive and loving qualities of your parents and mentors.

Prayer Suggestions
Imagine God like a loving parent, holding you close and telling you how deeply you're loved. God tells you he loves you no matter what. As a child rests in the arms of Mom or Dad, relax in the embrace of your loving God.

- *How have you experienced God's unconditional love in your life?*

Hallowed be thy name; thy kingdom come...

Usually, when we imagine the reign of God, we think of a place very far away from our everyday lives. God, however, asks us to begin the awesome task of building that kingdom here on earth!

Through our loving words and actions, we can usher in the reign of God here and now. This includes keeping the name of God holy and showing others how much reverence his name deserves. Jesus has given each of us a mission for the reign of God: "Go into the whole world and proclaim the gospel to every creature" (Mark 16:15).

Prayer Suggestions
Think about the next hour of your life. What will you be doing? Think of ways that you can bring the reign of God to your corner of the world in the next hour. How can your interactions with others be more Christlike?

- *What gifts or talents have you been given by God? How can you use them to build up God's kingdom?*
- *How do you see other people in your community building the kingdom of God? Your country? The world?*

Thy will be done on earth as it is in heaven...

Jesus came to reveal God's boundless, limitless love. God's love shined through his every action. As we work to do God's will on earth, we pray his heavenly love will shine through us, too.

Prayer Suggestions
Look back over your life. Can you see how your joys, sufferings, and failures are connected to your relationship with God and forming who you are? Can you thank God for the good and ask forgiveness for the bad?

- *What obstacles to doing God's will do you face?*
- *What events in the past week really showcased God's love for you?*

Give us this day our daily bread...

According to some biblical scholars, in this phrase Jesus is calling us to trust him to take care of our needs (remember that our needs are different from our wants). Catholics especially profess that Christ himself is our bread of eternal life; he is our "food for the journey."

- Give participants time to answer the other reflection question on their own.

Thy will be done on earth as it is in heaven.

- As a group, discuss events from the past week from the news, online, or in participants' own lives that were examples of God's will being done on earth. Have participants keep a list in their prayer journal. Then have participants answer the reflection questions on their own.

Prayer Suggestions

The next time you're at Mass, reflect on how Christ satisfies our spiritual hunger with the gifts of his Body and Blood in the Eucharist. Receiving holy Communion transforms us into new reflections of the body of Christ. Jesus is present in the world through our presence to our sisters and brothers.

Forgive us our trespasses as we forgive those who trespass against us...

In this phrase, we acknowledge that we've done wrong, we've sinned, but we also acknowledge God's great mercy when we beg for forgiveness. We are not only forgiven by God, but we're called to forgive those who hurt us as well:

"If you forgive others their transgressions, your heavenly Father will forgive you. But if you do not forgive others, neither will your Father forgive your transgressions."

Matthew 6:14–15

True forgiveness can be difficult, and sometimes it's a process that begins with just the desire to forgive (or sometimes even just the desire to desire to forgive).

Prayer Suggestions

Take a minute and think if there's someone you need to forgive or seek forgiveness from. Then take the time to write out what you'd like to say to that person. If you can, set up a time to talk with this person face to face or send her or him the letter and invite the person to meet later.

If it's impossible to send the letter or if meeting in person would put you in danger, keep the letter and share it with God in prayer. Trust that the grace of God's mercy and forgiveness is strong enough to cover you both—even from a distance.

And lead us not into temptation, but deliver us from evil.

It's easy for us to get lost, to fail, to slip into a sudden weakness. We face a tremendous number of temptations every day. In our search for who we are, we must constantly make decisions that can have lasting repercussions. We may be encouraged to do things we know are wrong. We may be ridiculed for doing what's right. We are tempted. We have to choose.

God can guide us in our decision making. When we're open to God's voice and willing to do what God tells us, God can keep us on the right path.

Prayer Suggestions

Pray with faith that God's power may free you from any sinfulness that controls your life. As you pray, imagine the light of Jesus filling the dark places within you. Recite the following prayer, mentioning and perhaps writing on the horizontal line the areas where you need God's help (for example, my pride, my stubbornness, my anger). Repeat as many times as you need to.

Come, Lord Jesus, shine the light of your glory

on: _____

The peace that Jesus offers his followers is his own peace, which flows from his intimate union with the Father. This peace does not leave us during times of temptation, loneliness, or low self-esteem. It does not leave us when we feel completely lost. Even when we really mess up, Jesus still offers his light and his peace. He longs for us to turn back to him.

In fact, sometimes we come to know Jesus best during the darkest, most difficult times of our lives. It is Jesus who helps bear the burden of our heavy cross. It is Jesus who carries us, lifting us up into the arms of our *Abba*.

Forgive us our trespasses as we forgive those who trespass against us.

- Ask participants what they think "trespasses" means in context. If they're having trouble with the definition, let them know that "trespass" means to sin, offend, hurt, or wound. So that this line is asking God to forgive us for the times we've sinned, hurting God, others, and ourselves, but also for the strength to forgive those who have hurt us.

And lead us not into temptation, but deliver us from evil.

- As a group, collect a list of areas where people commonly need God's help (overcoming pride, stubbornness, anger, seeking or giving forgiveness, etc.) Once you have a substantial list, recite the prayer from the **Prayer Suggestions** as a group until you've mentioned every item on your list.

- Then end your discussion of the Lord's Prayer with a strong "Amen."

With a partner or on your own, pick a line from the Lord's Prayer that stood out to you or that you found challenging. Then create an image, story, dialogue, etc., that shows what it means to really live this line.

With a partner or on your own, pick a line from the Lord's Prayer that stood out to you or that you found challenging. Then create an image, story, dialogue, or some other vehicle that shows what it means to really live this line.

JOURNEY OF FAITH

ENLIGHTENMENT

Reflect on a time in your life during which Jesus lifted you up.

What did that mean to you?

How can you offer that kind of support to someone else?

Journey of Faith for Teens: Enlightenment. E6 (826313)
Imprimi Potest: Stephen T. Rehrauer, CSsR, Provincial, Denver Province, the Redemptorists.
Imprimatur: "In accordance with CIC 827, permission to publish has been granted on June 30, 2016, by the Rev. Msgr. Mark S. Rivituso, Vicar General, Archdiocese of St. Louis. Permission to publish is an indication that nothing contrary to Church teaching is contained in this work. It does not imply any endorsement of the opinions expressed in the publication, nor is any liability assumed by this permission."
Journey of Faith for Teens © 2000, 2016 Liguori Publications, Liguori, MO 63057. All rights reserved. No part of this publication may be reproduced, distributed, stored, transmitted, or posted in any form by any means without prior written permission. To order, visit Liguori.org or call 800-325-9521 Liguori Publications, a nonprofit corporation, is an apostolate of the Redemptorists. To learn more about the Redemptorists, visit Redemptorists.com. Editors of 2016 edition: Theresa Nienaber and Pat Fosarelli, MD, DMin. Design: Lorena Mitre Jimenez. Images: Shutterstock.
Scripture texts in this work are taken from the *New American Bible*, revised edition © 2010, 1991, 1986, 1970 Confraternity of Christian Doctrine, Washington, D.C., and are used by permission of the copyright owner. All Rights Reserved. No part of the *New American Bible* may be reproduced in any form without permission in writing from the copyright owner. Excerpts from English translation of the *Catechism of the Catholic Church for the United States of America* © 1994 United States Catholic Conference, Inc.—Libreria Editrice Vaticana; English translation of the *Catechism of the Catholic Church: Modifications from the Editio Typica* © 1997 United States Catholic Conference, Inc.—Libreria Editrice Vaticana. Compliant with *The Roman Missal, Third Edition*.
Printed in the United States of America. 20 19 18 17 16 / 5 4 3 2 1. Third Edition.

Liguori
PUBLICATIONS
A Redemptorist Ministry

Journaling

Reflect on a time in your life during which Jesus lifted you up. What did that mean to you? How can you offer that kind of support to someone else?

Closing Prayer

Ask the participants to spend several moments in silence, bringing to mind problems, worries, burdens, and special intentions. Ask them to imagine placing these burdens in the arms of the loving and compassionate Father. Close the lesson by asking participants to continue in silent prayer, this time thanking the Father for people, events, and things for which they are most grateful. End with the sign of the cross.

Take-Home

Ask participants to find time between now and their next session to reflect on how God has been a father to them during their RCIA journey.

Catechism: 605–655

Objectives

- Recall the major events of Jesus' final days through his resurrection.

- Recognize that Palm Sunday and the Easter Triduum mark the main events of Holy Week.

- Identify our call to share the good news of Jesus' resurrection with others as being entrusted to us by Jesus.

Leader Meditation

A Catechist's Personal Prayer

As you prepare your group for the Easter Vigil, pray the following for strength and your own spiritual growth:

Me! A spiritual companion for fledgling faith! Loving Spirit of God, I tremble inside. I hold fast to you, great Giver of Life, offering my prayer of thanksgiving for this very special gift, and my prayer of supplication for the graces needed to be worthy of it. Can anything be more important than being a good catechist for one who is about to enter your Church? Overwhelmed by the honor of it and frightened by the responsibility of it, I say,

"Yes, my Lord. It is not clear why you have chosen me, but you clearly have. So I will travel this journey of faith with the ones you entrusted to my care. We will share our stories, and will learn more of you as we learn more of ourselves, through the eyes of always-newly becoming Christian witness. Grant all of us the grace to touch each other's hearts with your tender mercy and your steadfast love. Amen.

Leader Preparation

- Read the lesson, this lesson plan, the Scripture passage, and the *Catechism* sections.

- Be familiar with the vocabulary terms for this lesson: chrism Mass, holy chrism, oil of catechumens, oil of the infirm, Mass of the Lord's Supper. Definitions are provided in this guide's glossary.

Welcome

Greet participants as they arrive. Check for supplies and immediate needs. Solicit questions or comments about the previous sessions and/or share new information and findings. Begin promptly.

Opening Scripture

John 13:1–15

Ask one of the participants to light the candle and read aloud. Before beginning your discussion of the lesson handout, ask participants to think about **what Jesus' command for us to wash each other's feet means for us today**.

> "Therefore Easter is not simply one feast among others, but the 'Feast of feasts,' the 'Solemnity of solemnities.'"
>
> *CCC 1169*

Journey of Faith

In Short:

- During Holy Week, we follow the events of Jesus' passion through his resurrection.
- Palm Sunday and the Easter Triduum mark the main events of Holy Week.
- Jesus entrusts us with sharing the good news of his resurrection with others.

The Meaning of Holy Week

Imagine you are one of Jesus' disciples. You have witnessed miracles. You have heard the message of God's great kindness and mercy, and you have seen Jesus live that message in his own life. He wasn't the Messiah you expected, but you believe he is who he claims to be. You believe Jesus is the Messiah. You believe he is the Son of God.

Then one night he washes your feet in an act of intimate service and shares a meal with you. Then he is taken from you by an angry crowd after being betrayed by one of his friends. He is beaten. He is ridiculed. He is hanged from a cross with common criminals.

> - How would you react to Jesus' crucifixion? How hard or easy would it be to hold on to hope?

During Holy Week, we enter into Christ's passion, death, and resurrection. We not only think about these important events of salvation in a historical way but we also celebrate them in a sacramental way that makes these sacred mysteries present to us.

Palm Sunday

Holy Week begins on Palm Sunday of the Passion of the Lord, the Sunday before Easter. This liturgy recalls Jesus' dramatic entrance into Jerusalem. He came humbly, riding on a donkey, yet he was honored by the people as the Son of David, the heir to the kingdom. The people laid palm branches before him, greeting Jesus in the spirit of joy and triumph usually associated with victorious kings and armies.

> *"On the next day, when the great crowd that had come to the feast heard that Jesus was coming to Jerusalem, they took palm branches and went out to meet him."*
>
> *John 12:12–13*

After hearing this story from one of the Gospels, we take up our own palm branches and sing, celebrating and honoring Christ our king as the congregation processes into the church. Later, we hear the story of Jesus' passion. These same people who welcomed him in Jerusalem ask for his crucifixion less than a week later. Through these two stories we reflect on the weakness of our human nature.

CCC 605–655

Palm Sunday

- As you discuss Palm Sunday, share that many Catholics save the palms and present them for burning prior to Ash Wednesday the following year. Last year's palms provided the ashes for this year's Ash Wednesday.

- Discuss with participants how the readings on Palm Sunday show our human nature.

Suggested responses include: First we hear about Jesus' entrance into Jerusalem where he's honored as a king, then we hear about his crucifixion. We see the good and bad sides of our human nature (treating Jesus as king, but then condemning him to the cross with our sins).

The Meaning of Holy Week

- Give participants time to answer the reflection question on their own.

- Emphasize that Holy Week helps us understand the meaning behind and reality of these historic events.

- Ask participants if there's anything they've noticed about the church building that's different during Lent than it has been. Are there any special events the parish offers that only occur during Lent? (If you know of things the participants don't list, take the time to share those now.)

- As you talk about the days of Holy Week, share how your parish celebrates each of these special feasts.

Holy Thursday

- Discuss why Jesus might have commanded his disciples to wash the feet of others on the same night he instituted the holy Eucharist.

Suggested responses include: Jesus was handing down his ministry, he wanted to emphasize the disciples were servants of his Body, he wanted to show that all his actions are in service of the Body of Christ including his death, etc.

Serve Like Jesus

- Recall or, if you have time, reread the Scripture passage about the washing of the feet you read at the beginning of this session.

- Allow time for participants to respond to the reflection questions. Ask volunteers to share their responses.

Good Friday

- Discuss with participants how Good Friday might have been different for Jesus' followers who did not know he was going to come back from the dead three days later.

Suggested responses include: They would have been scared, they would have been sad, they might have lost faith, they might have doubted Jesus was really God, etc.

- Give participants time to respond to the reflection questions. Ask volunteers to share their responses.

The Easter Triduum

Triduum means "a three-day festival." It's a time set aside for prayer and worship. The Easter Triduum comprises three days—Holy Thursday, Good Friday, and the Easter Vigil on Saturday, the heart and core of the whole Church year.

Holy Thursday

The Triduum begins the evening of Holy Thursday, when the **Mass of the Lord's Supper** celebrates our Lord's founding or institution of the holy Eucharist. In fact, Holy Thursday is the feast day of the Eucharist and the priesthood. Traditionally in the morning (before the official start of the Triduum), priests and people gather with their bishops for the great chrism Mass. The priests renew their commitment to priestly service, and the people are asked to pray for them.

The three sacred oils used in the Church are blessed by the bishops during the Chrism Mass:

- **The holy chrism** is used in the sacraments of baptism, confirmation, and holy orders as well as during a church's dedication ceremony.
- **The oil of catechumens** is used during baptism and during the period of the catechumenate.
- **The oil of the infirm** is used in the sacrament of anointing of the sick.

After reading about Jesus' command to serve others as he has served, the celebrant washes the feet of twelve people, representing the twelve apostles whose feet Jesus washed at the Last Supper. This action reflects Jesus' teaching that true leadership means service. At the end of the Mass, a procession takes the Blessed Sacrament from the main tabernacle to a smaller altar of repose.

Serve Like Jesus

"I have given you a model to follow, so that as I have done for you, you should also do."

John 13:15

Read John 13:1–15. Imagine the scene as if you're there; as if Jesus is washing *your* feet.

- How do you feel about Jesus washing your feet? Uncomfortable? Embarrassed? Amazed?
- How is Jesus asking you to serve others in your life?

Good Friday

The central act of worship on Good Friday is the celebration of the passion of the Lord. This celebration has three key parts:

- Reading the story of the passion from John's Gospel during the Liturgy of the Word, followed by prayers for the Church and the world.
- The adoration or veneration of the cross. The cross is always a symbol of our salvation and a sign of God's love for us; during Good Friday we make an additional display of our reverence for the cross to show how grateful we are for Christ's perfect sacrifice.
- Good Friday is the only day of the Church year where we don't celebrate a full Mass, but we can still receive holy Communion, in the form of bread only, which has been reserved from Mass on Holy Thursday.

Good Friday is a day of serious reflection on what Christ's death means for us. We are called to both abstain from meat and fast on this Friday as another way to bring us closer to Christ's suffering. Many Catholics also celebrate the Way of the Cross on Good Friday afternoon (see *E5: The Way of the Cross*). This reflection isn't meant to depress us. Rather, we reflect on Christ's death as a way of acknowledging his sacrifice and that Christ's sacrifice was necessary for us to have eternal life with him.

- How does your belief in Christ's victory over death change how you think about death?

- What would it be like to face death without faith?

Holy Saturday

During the day, the Church is silent and the altars are bare. The tabernacle is empty. This symbolizes how we are waiting in silence at the tomb for our Lord's resurrection. We've prepared for the Easter sacraments through prayer, reflection, and fasting.

After sunset, the church explodes into joy! The celebration of Jesus' resurrection begins. "This is the night when Christ broke the prison bars of death," proclaims the Church in the Proclamation of Easter. And what a night it is! This is a night for the whole parish to celebrate with Catholic churches throughout the world. We come together for the Easter Vigil to experience the central message of our faith—that Jesus is risen and that death and sin are conquered.

The vigil begins at the door of the darkened church, where new fire is kindled. The priest blesses the paschal candle and lights it from the Easter fire. The celebrant or a deacon holds the candle high and carries it into the church, proclaiming, "The Light of Christ!" We respond, "Thanks be to God!" Other candles are lit from the paschal candle until light fills the whole church, a vibrant symbol of how the light of Christ dispels our darkness.

The Liturgy of the Word leads us to reflect on God's faithful love throughout salvation history. Up to seven Old Testament readings are proclaimed, with psalms interspersed. We listen to the epistle from Romans in which St. Paul writes about our being buried with Jesus Christ "through baptism into death, so that, just as Christ was raised from the dead by the glory of the Father, we too might live in newness of life" (6:4). We sing the "Alleluia" for the first time since Lent began. The Gospel and homily follow.

Catechumens are called forth for baptism. We pray a Litany of the Saints. The priest blesses the water. The catechumens are baptized, clothed in white garments, and given lighted candles. The assembly renews their baptismal vows.

Candidates for full communion make a profession of faith. They join the newly baptized for confirmation and later receive first Eucharist.

As with every Mass, we are sent forth to be Christ's body in the world. The Mass ends, but the journey of new Catholics has just begun.

Easter Sunday

Easter morning follows. New life and fresh hope have come in the risen Christ. We celebrate with a renewal of our baptismal promises to reject sin and evil, to love God, and to follow Jesus. But the celebration isn't over!

Easter Sunday marks the beginning of the Easter season—a fifty-day celebration in the Church year that continues until Pentecost. Joyful music, bright spring flowers, and renewed faith in the risen Lord fill the liturgies of this season.

Holy Saturday

- Emphasize the importance of the Holy Saturday celebration and the participants' personal involvement. Discuss the meaning of the powerful symbols: light, water, oil, and the cross, that they will see on Holy Saturday.

- Open up the discussion to participants' questions about what will happen during the Easter Vigil Mass.

The light shows how the light of Christ dispels our darkness, the water symbolizes how we are cleansed of our sins in baptism, the oil that we are anointed as followers of Christ, and the cross is the symbol of Christ's glorious death and resurrection.

Refer back to the reflection at the beginning of this handout. Imagine you are that follower of Jesus, except this time you are hearing the good news of Jesus' resurrection. With a partner or on your own, create your reaction to this news. It can be a story, poem, picture, skit, or anything else you can think of.

Refer back to the reflection at the beginning of this handout. Imagine you are that follower of Jesus, except this time you are hearing the good news of Jesus' resurrection. With a partner or on your own, create your reaction to this news (it can be a story, poem, picture, skit, or anything else you can think of).

The resurrection story may also occur in our personal lives. Perhaps we have lost a friend and have felt we would die from heartache or loneliness, only to find that our letting go allowed us to enter into a new relationship that was uniquely life-giving and positive. *Write about a time when part of you (or part of your life) had to die so that a new life could begin.*

Journey of Faith for Teens: Enlightenment, E7 (826313)
Imprimi Potest: Stephen T. Rehrauer, CSsR, Provincial, Denver Province, the Redemptorists.
Imprimatur: "In accordance with CIC 827, permission to publish has been granted on June 30, 2016, by the Rev. Msgr. Mark S. Rivituso, Vicar General, Archdiocese of St. Louis. Permission to publish is an indication that nothing contrary to Church teaching is contained in this work. It does not imply any endorsement of the opinions expressed in the publication; nor is any liability assumed by this permission."
Journey of Faith for Teens © 2000, 2016 Liguori Publications, Liguori, MO 63057. All rights reserved. No part of this publication may be reproduced, distributed, stored, transmitted, or posted in any form by any means without prior written permission. To order, visit Liguori.org or call 800-325-9521. Liguori Publications, a nonprofit corporation, is an apostolate of the Redemptorists. To learn more about the Redemptorists, visit Redemptorists.com. Editors of 2016 edition: Theresa Nienaber and Pat Fosarelli, MD, DMin. Design: Lorena Mitre Jimenez. Images: Shutterstock.
Scripture texts in this work are taken from the *New American Bible*, revised edition © 2010, 1991, 1986, 1970 Confraternity of Christian Doctrine, Washington, D.C., and are used by permission of the copyright owner. All Rights Reserved. No part of the *New American Bible* may be reproduced in any form without permission in writing from the copyright owner. Excerpts from English translation of the *Catechism of the Catholic Church* for the United States of America © 1994 United States Catholic Conference, Inc. —*Libreria Editrice Vaticana*. English translation of the *Catechism of the Catholic Church: Modifications from the Editio Typica* © 1997 United States Catholic Conference, Inc. —*Libreria Editrice Vaticana*. Compliant with The Roman Missal, Third Edition.
Printed in the United States of America. 20 19 18 17 16 / 5 4 3 2 1. Third Edition.

Liguori
PUBLICATIONS
A Redemptorist Ministry

Journaling

The resurrection story may also occur in our personal lives. Perhaps we have lost a friend and have felt we would die from heartache or loneliness, only to find that our letting go enabled us to enter into a new relationship that was uniquely life-giving and positive. *Write about a time when part of you (or part of your life) had to die so that a new life could begin.*

Closing Prayer

As a group, pray:

Good and gracious Lord Jesus Christ, we love you. We praise you. We adore you. You have guided us on our faith journey, and now we are preparing to receive your graces through the sacraments. You are our Lord and Creator. You formed each one of us. Shine your love upon us so we may continue to know you and love you in return. Amen.

Take-Home

Ask participants to think about the joy the disciples must have felt at Jesus' resurrection, then encourage them to bring that same joy into their everyday lives and share it with everyone they meet.

Objectives

- Recall that their journey through RCIA involved growing in love of God and his Church.

- Reflect on the RCIA journey of participants through the Easter Vigil readings.

- Realize initiation into the Church is just the beginning of an ongoing formation.

Leader Meditation

Gather with those leading the retreat, the hospitality team, and your parish priest just prior to the arrival of the candidates and catechumens. Read and reflect on Psalm 92—"It is good to give thanks to the LORD!"

Voice any special intentions, including the success of this Retreat Day. Conclude by praying the Lord's Prayer together or asking for a priestly blessing.

Prepare to welcome the retreatants.

Leader Preparation

- Read the lesson, this lesson plan, the Scripture passage, and the *Catechism* sections.

- The end of this retreat is a good time to offer the sacrament of penance and reconciliation. Talk to your parish priest and see if this is a possibility.

- This retreat is based on the Easter Vigil Liturgy of the Word. There are retreat activities for all nine possible readings, but you may not have time for all of them. Find out which readings will be used in your parish for the Easter Vigil and choose among those activities for the retreat.

- Ideally, the retreat should take place at a retreat center or facility that has an outdoor area where retreatants can walk around safely. If this isn't possible, try to host the retreat where the participants still have room to spread out or walk even if it's all inside.

- Prayer journals (invite participants to bring their own)

- Small pieces of paper and a small fireproof bowl or urn

- One flower for each participant

- Nametags for everyone participating in the retreat, including leaders and the hospitality team

- Refreshments (snacks, drinks, and food for a light lunch)

- Sponsor and secret intercessor letters for participants

- Bibles

Welcome

Greet participants as they arrive. Alert them to any materials they'll need to start the retreat and encourage them to fill out a nametag.

Opening Prayer

Pray the prayer that appears in the E8 lesson handout together:

Lord Jesus Christ, open our minds and hearts to your presence today. Guide us as we journey through this process, and bring us closer to you each day. Help us know you better, and help us see your goodness in everyone we meet. Amen.

Journey of Faith

In Short:

- Your journey through the RCIA involves growing in love of God and his Church.
- The Scripture readings from the Easter Vigil help us reflect on this journey.
- Initiation into the Church is the beginning of an ongoing formation.

Easter Vigil Retreat

You've come a long way on your journey of faith. You've become part of a faith community, you've grown in knowledge of God, and you've taken a closer look at yourself and your faith. You've been preparing for the next step—initiation into the Church and reception of the sacraments.

The reflections and activities during this time of reflection and sharing will help you prepare in heart and spirit for the celebration of Christ's resurrection and the next stage of your faith journey.

Opening Prayer

Lord, open our minds and hearts to your presence today. Guide us as we journey through this process and bring us closer to you each day. Help us know you better and help us see your goodness in everyone we meet. Amen.

First Reading: Genesis 1:1—2:2

"God looked at everything he had made, and found it very good."

Genesis 1:31

Spend time alone outside. Walk around and take in everything you see. God is present in this creation. If an object or a scene catches your eye, reflect on it. What is God trying to reveal to you?

A plant growing through a cracked stone might be a reminder that your faith is strong enough to grow through tough times. A seedpod might be a reminder of how important it is to have patience as you work on your spiritual growth. A sturdy oak tree might show how strong you can become when rooted in Christ.

If you can't get outside, imagine your favorite outdoor spot. What about this place makes it so important to you? Where do you find God there?

- What can you learn about God through his creations?

Second Reading: Genesis 22:1–18

"God put Abraham to the test and said to him: Abraham! 'Here I am!' he replied."

Genesis 22:1

Easter Vigil Retreat

First Reading: Genesis 1:1—2:2, activity, and reflection

Follow this reading with a ten-minute talk by a convert from a previous RCIA group. The talk should focus on personal experience, and how grace can become a catalyst for conversion or ongoing conversion. End with a prayer or silent meditation.

Second Reading: Genesis 22:1–18, activity, and reflection

After the reading, have participants answer the reflection questions on a small sheet of paper. Once that's been completed, designate a leader to call out the name of each catechumenate and candidate. After their name is called, the participant should answer "Here I am!" as Abraham did, come forward, and place their piece of paper in the ceramic bowl. After all the names have been called, safely burn the papers. If you can't burn the papers safely, shred them or dispose of them later.

Third Reading: Exodus 14:15—15:1, activity, and reflection

Follow the third reading with a ten-minute talk by a convert from a previous RCIA group. The talk should emphasize an experience in which the convert was guided through a difficult time and how God was present during this time. End with a prayer or silent meditation.

Allow time for a short break.

Fourth Reading: Isaiah 54:5–14, activity, and reflection

If you collected letters from participants' sponsors, family members, friends, or secret intercessors pass out those letters now and give participants the opportunity to read and respond to those letters.

If you don't have letters to share with participants, follow the fourth reading with a ten-minute talk by a convert from a previous RCIA group. This talk should emphasize the ways the conversion process made the divine love real for this new Catholic.

Fifth Reading: Isaiah 55:1–11, activity, and reflection

Follow the fifth reading with a ten-minute talk by a convert from a previous RCIA group. This talk should recall a story of discernment and change as RCIA classes ended and the speaker was called to begin a new life in Christ. End with a prayer or silent meditation.

How eagerly do you answer God's call? Do you shout, "Here I am!" like Abraham? Or are you less eager, responding "Can you come back when it's more convenient?" Or "I'm willing, but only if...."

God has given Abraham so much, but now God is asking: *Do you trust me? Are you really ready to answer my call?* As you look forward to entering the Church, God is asking you these questions as well.

> • Look back on your journey through the RCIA process. What has God called you to sacrifice? (a habit that wasn't Christian? A way of thinking? Time spent doing other things to commit to Mass and the RCIA? Friends who didn't support your decision or were a bad influence?)
>
> • What have you gained through this sacrifice or offering?

Third Reading: Exodus 14:15—15:1

"Then the LORD said to Moses:...'Lift up your staff and stretch out your hand over the sea, and split it in two, that the Israelites may pass through the sea on dry land.'"

Exodus 14:15–16

This reading shows how God has worked many miracles for his Chosen People, and God is still working miracles for each of us. Your journey through the RCIA process is something like the Israelites' journey out of Egypt. God has called you out of slavery to sin and into the freedom of a loving God. As you decided to start the RCIA, as you've grown and changed, God has been there to guide and protect you.

That guidance and protection doesn't end with the RCIA, either. God will continue to guide and protect you as you start your life as a member of his Church.

> • How have you, or how has your faith, changed since the beginning the RCIA?
>
> • What was the most wonderful thing God did for you on this journey?
>
> • What was the most difficult part of the journey? How did God guide you through it?

Fourth Reading: Isaiah 54:5–14

"Though the mountains fall away and the hills be shaken, My love shall never fall away from you nor my covenant of peace be shaken, says the LORD, who has mercy on you."

Isaiah 54:10

This reading is a love letter from God. God is pictured as a friend, a spouse who wants to repair any damage done to our relationship and shower us with love.

In this reading God is not a parent or a judge but a beloved friend who is asking us to share our lives with him. Sharing our lives with God isn't always easy. It means admitting and asking forgiveness for the times we sin. It means humbly accepting God's plan for our lives. It means making the right decisions even when we struggle or the decision is unpopular. But in return, we get a lifetime of love.

> • Are there any relationships in your life that come close to the relationship described in the reading? If yes, how have they changed your life? If not, how could a relationship like this be life-changing?
>
> • How does this reading from Isaiah change the way you view God?
>
> • How would your life be different if you lived every day with this image of God in mind?

Fifth Reading: Isaiah 55:1–11

"So shall my word be that goes forth from my mouth; It shall not return to me empty, but shall do what pleases me, achieving the end for which I sent it."

Isaiah 55:11

This reading speaks about the power of God's word.

Take your Bible and spend quiet time contemplating this reading on your own. To allow the words to sink in, reread each verse as many times as you need to. Be aware of your reactions. Is there a verse that seems to speak directly to you? Is there a verse you find yourself resisting or pushing against?

Take these reactions, positive and negative, to prayer. Thank God for the words you find comforting, for the verses you see your life reflected in. Ask God for help with those verses you have trouble understanding. Allow God to open your heart to the verses you find uncomfortable.

Then read the verses again, but this time when you're finished reading, sit in silence with God's word. Give God a chance to respond in your heart.

- How can you take what you've learned into your life outside of your RCIA sessions?

Sixth Reading: Baruch 3:9–15, 32—4:4

"Blessed are we, O Israel; for what pleases God is known to us!"

Baruch 4:4

This reading talks about God's wisdom which, as we know, isn't always the same as the wisdom of the world. Saint Paul tells us that the wisdom of God can often seem foolish to those of us who look for worldly approval or worldly success. The Christian perspective is often much different than the world's perspective.

In your journal or with a partner, take time to make a list of worldly wisdom. Then alongside it, write what God's wisdom is, using Scripture if you can. For example, worldly wisdom might say "your value as a person is determined by what you're worth in dollars." But God's wisdom says: "Do not store up for yourselves treasures on earth....But store up treasures in heaven, where neither moth nor decay destroys, nor thieves break in and steal" (Matthew 6:19–20). Keep in mind, while often different, you may find some values of the world and of God that align. Don't be afraid to add these to your list, too.

Seventh Reading: Ezekiel 36:16–28

"I will give you a new heart, and a new spirit I will put within you. I will remove the heart of stone from your flesh and give you a heart of flesh."

Ezekiel 36:26

A Meditation

Sit comfortably and away from distractions. Close your eyes or focus your gaze on a sacred object like a crucifix that will keep you focused on God.

Now breathe in and out slowly. With each breath, imagine yourself moving down to the center of yourself, to your heart. Push away any distracting thoughts and continue to breathe slowly in and out. Ask God to show you your heart. How has it changed through the RCIA process? In what ways does it still need to grow?

Now imagine that God is creating a new heart within you. What is this new heart like? How does this new heart make you feel?

- Think about your old heart and your new heart. How are they the same? How are they different? (If you prefer, draw the two hearts and include their similarities and differences.)

Epistle: Romans 6:3–11

"We were indeed buried with him through baptism into death, so that, just as Christ was raised from the dead by the glory of the Father, we too might live in newness of life."

Romans 6:4

- In baptism, we die with Christ. It is natural to be afraid of change. What fears do you have about the changes baptism or entry into the Catholic Church will make in your life?
- In baptism, we are raised with Christ. What hopes do you have about your future in the Church?

Meditation

This would be a good opportunity to move the retreat into the parish church (if you're not already there) and offer catechumens the opportunity to receive the sacrament of penance and reconciliation. Offer candidates a quiet space to reflect on an examination of conscience. If you can, also allow this time for adoration of the Blessed Sacrament as candidates participate in reconciliation. Participants can use the guided meditation in the lesson handout, or prayer on their own during this time.

Epistle: Romans 6:3–11

When all candidates who wish to receive reconciliation have done so, allow a final moment of silence before reading the epistle.

Sixth Reading: Baruch 3:8–15, 32–44, activity, and reflection

Follow the sixth reading with a ten-minute talk by a convert from a previous RCIA group. This talk should describe how the person's wisdom changed as he or she grew in the Catholic faith. End with a prayer or silent meditation.

Break for lunch.

Seventh Reading: Ezekiel 36:16–28, activity, and reflection

Follow the seventh reading with a ten-minute talk by a catechumen/candidate from a previous RCIA group. This talk should be a personal witness to the changes that occurred in the convert's heart as he or she grew in the faith.

Gospel:
Matthew 28:1–10 (year A);
Mark 16:1–7 (year B);
Luke 24:1–12 (year C)

If a priest is available, have him read the Gospel from the altar and offer a short homily for the participants on the blessing of Christ's presence in their lives.

ENLIGHTENMENT

JOURNEY OF FAITH

Gospel:
Year A, Matthew 28:1–10;
Year B, Mark 16:1–7;
Year C, Luke 24:1–12

*"You seek Jesus of Nazareth, the crucified.
He has been raised; he is not here."*

Mark 16:6

- *Reflect on the miracle of Christ's resurrection, Christ's promise to you, and Christ's presence in your life.*

- *What do these things mean to you?*

Closing Prayer

Lord Jesus, you are the resurrection and the life. We have journeyed from darkness to light, from being alone to belonging, from doubt to faith. Guide us on the next step of our journey to make a commitment—a covenant with the living God—Father, Son, and Holy Spirit. Amen.

Journey of Faith for Teens: Enlightenment, E8 (826313)

Imprimi Potest: Stephen T. Rehrauer, CSsR, Provincial, Denver Province, the Redemptorists.

Imprimatur: "In accordance with CIC 827, permission to publish has been granted on June 30, 2016, by the Rev. Msgr. Mark S. Rivituso, Vicar General, Archdiocese of St. Louis. Permission to publish is an indication that nothing contrary to Church teaching is contained in this work. It does not imply any endorsement of the opinions expressed in the publication; nor is any liability assumed by this permission."

Journey of Faith for Teens © 2000, 2016 Liguori Publications, Liguori, MO 63057 All rights reserved. No part of this publication may be reproduced, distributed, stored, transmitted, or posted in any form by any means without prior written permission. To order, visit Liguori.org or call 800-325-9521. Liguori Publications, a nonprofit corporation, is an apostolate of the Redemptorists. To learn more about the Redemptorists, visit Redemptorists.com. Editors of 2016 edition: Theresa Nienaber and Pat Fosarelli, MD, DMin. Design: Lorena Mitre Jimenez. Images: Shutterstock.

Scripture texts in this work are taken from the *New American Bible*, revised edition © 2010, 1991, 1986, 1970 Confraternity of Christian Doctrine, Washington, D.C., and are used by permission of the copyright owner. All Rights Reserved. No part of the *New American Bible* may be reproduced in any form without permission in writing from the copyright owner. Excerpts from English translation of the *Catechism of the Catholic Church for the United States of America* © 1994 United States Catholic Conference, Inc.—*Libreria Editrice Vaticana*; English translation of the *Catechism of the Catholic Church: Modifications from the Editio Typica* © 1997 United States Catholic Conference, Inc.—*Libreria Editrice Vaticana*. Compliant with *The Roman Missal, Third Edition*. Printed in the United States of America. 20 19 18 17 16 / 5 4 3 2 1. Third Edition.

Liguori
PUBLICATIONS
A Redemptorist Ministry

Closing Prayer

Pray together this prayer from the end of the E8 lesson handout:

Lord Jesus, you are the resurrection and the life. We have journeyed from darkness to light, from being alone to belonging, from doubt to faith. Guide us on the next step of our journey to make a commitment—a covenant with the living God—Father, Son, and Holy Spirit. Amen.

Looking Ahead

Provide participants with any specific instructions or information they need before the Easter Vigil. Remind them that they will enter the final stage, Mystagogy, after Easter.

M1: Conversion: A Lifelong Process

Catechism: 160, 545, 981, 1427–29

Objectives

- Describe conversion as an ongoing and lifelong process.

- Identify God's grace and continued perseverance as necessary for spiritual growth.

- Recognize participation is an important part of our community faith.

Leader Meditation

Acts 2:42–47

The new believer is filled with awe and called to share and serve with others. This is what your participants are called to do during the period of mystagogy. Through the sacraments, the Holy Spirit has filled them so abundantly with grace that it is overflowing, enabling them to perform good works for the kingdom of God. God has already done this in your own life. Now he is doing it in the lives of the neophytes entrusted to your care. Pray for the continued outpouring of the Holy Spirit and the manifestation of the gifts received at confirmation.

Leader Preparation

- Read the lesson, this lesson plan, the Scripture passage, and the Catechism sections.

- Be familiar with the vocabulary terms for this lesson: mystagogy, neophytes, conversion, initial conversion. Definitions are provided in this guide's glossary.

- Find a recording of an Easter song to use for the closing prayer.

Welcome

Greet neophytes as they arrive. Check for supplies and immediate needs. Solicit questions or comments about the previous sessions and/or share new information and findings. Begin promptly.

Opening Scripture

Acts 2:42–47

Ask a volunteer to light the candle and read aloud. Ask participants to imagine they are part of the early Church and witnesses to the spreading of the gospel message. Do they have the same sense of awe that the first disciples experienced? Are they filled with a desire to serve others? Before beginning your discussion of the lesson handout, ***ask participants to hold on to these questions as you discuss the lesson handout.***

> "Christ's call to conversion continues to resound in the lives of Christians. This second conversion is an uninterrupted task for the whole Church."
>
> CCC 1428

Journey of Faith

M1

In Short:

- Conversion is a lifelong process.
- God's grace and continued perseverance are needed for spiritual growth.
- Participation is an important part of our community faith.

- What role do you see your faith playing in your life?
- How will your life be different because of it?

Conversion: A Lifelong Process

Welcome! You're now a fully initiated member of the Catholic Church.

The Easter Vigil isn't the end of your formation as a Catholic. It actually marks the beginning of your commitment to learning more about and living out the Catholic Christian message. Your journey continues.

The next stage of the RCIA process is called **mystagogy**, a Greek word meaning "mystery." The early Church used the fifty days from Easter to Pentecost to explain the mystery of the sacraments celebrated at Easter. Today this post-Easter period serves a similar purpose. It's a time for **neophytes** (the newly baptized) to gain a deeper understanding of God's word, the sacraments, and what their new commitment means for their lives.

As you explore mystagogy, your focus will shift from learning about the faith to living the faith. You'll recommit to the Church every day you choose to live like Jesus.

Mountaintops and Valleys

"The soul of one who serves God always swims in joy, always keeps holiday, and is always in the mood for singing."

St. John of the Cross

You may be feeling what St. John of the Cross described. You may also be experiencing other feelings:

"I felt such a spiritual high during the Easter Vigil. But now everything else seems so...ordinary."

"I feel like I've graduated. I guess I don't have to keep coming to these meetings."

"I feel kind of confused. I spent so much energy preparing for initiation into the Church. Now what do I do?"

"I really love my new faith, but I still have questions. Maybe I should have waited."

Even the apostles weren't swimming in joy all the time. Peter experienced Jesus' transfiguration in person (Matthew 17:1–9) and wanted to stay on that mountaintop—but he had to come down. The joy of that mountaintop experience must have faded into the background as the apostles witnessed Jesus' suffering and death.

CCC 160, 545, 981, 1427–29

Conversion: A Lifelong Process

- Give participants time to answer the reflection questions on their own, then discuss as a group. Ask participants how they have changed now that they are part of the Church.

Mountaintops and Valleys

- Ask participants which of the comments in the handout best describes their own feelings now that they are fully initiated into the Church. If participants are reluctant to share, have them close their eyes and raise their hands when you read the comment that most closely matches their own experience.

- Emphasize that during the process of conversion there are many highs and lows. It isn't a steady process, and what they're experiencing now may change over time.

Ongoing Conversion

- Discuss the meaning of the word *conversion* and the difference between conversion and initial conversion. Ask participants how they feel about conversion now that their initial conversion is over and they are fully initiated into the Church.

- Give participants time to answer the reflection questions, and ask volunteers to share their response or share your own response to the last two questions.

How Will Ongoing Conversion Affect My Life?

- Ask participants how Alphonsus Liguori experienced initial conversion.

Suggested response includes: His initial conversion was when he went to church after an argument with his father and heard God literally calling him, "give yourself to me."

- Ask participants how St. Alphonsus experienced ongoing conversion.

Suggested responses includes He continued to grow in his faith, he continued to go where God called him, he learned more about God through his experiences, he used his gifts and talents to lead other people to God.

- Give participants time to answer the reflection questions and ask volunteers to share their response.

Whether you're still on that spiritual high or the newness is fading as you get back to life as usual, hold on to your desire to continue learning about the mysteries of faith. This is part of your ongoing conversion.

Ongoing Conversion

At its root, conversion means "to change or turn around." **Conversion** is the ever-present call of the Christian to grow in faith and to live out that faith. It means deepening our relationship with God and our fellow Christians.

The first step in the conversion process is to turn to Jesus Christ, accept him as Lord and Savior, and choose to live the life of faith in the community of God's people. This first step is called **initial conversion**. It may be a moving experience, a dramatic moment, or something that moves you deep in your soul. Or it may be subtle, a change that happens gradually.

- *Reflect on your own initial conversion. What was the turning point that made you want to know more? When did you know you were on the right path?*

Conversion is a process that requires nurturing and the right atmosphere to continue growing. Even Jesus' apostles continued to change and grow in faith after their initial conversion.

James and John were looking for a warrior king like those of the Old Testament who would rally the people, gather an army, and drive out the Romans. But Jesus came as the "suffering servant" (see Isaiah 53) and called his apostles "not to be served, but to serve" (Matthew 20:28). This wasn't at all what they expected, but as they followed Jesus they discovered that his mission of salvation was greater than any mission of conquest they had imagined.

> Indeed, Christ invited people to faith and conversion, but he never coerced them. "For he bore witness to the truth but refused to use force to impose it on those who spoke against it. His kingdom...grows by the love with which Christ, lifted up on the cross, draws men to himself."
>
> *CCC 160*

- *Have you ever experienced something that was better than you expected?*
- *How have your expectations of the Church changed as you've grown in faith?*
- *Has anything you've experienced in the Church been better than you expected?*

How Will Ongoing Conversion Affect My Life?

In the eighteenth century, Alphonsus Liguori, an ambitious young lawyer, was handling a complicated case between two Italian dukes. When he lost the case through deception, his whole world collapsed. He stormed out of the courtroom saying, "World, I know you now."

A few weeks later, after an argument with his domineering father, he walked into a church and heard a voice saying, "Alphonsus, give yourself to me." He went up the street to the church of Our Lady of Ransom and placed his sword, the symbol of his nobility, on one of the side altars—symbolizing his decision to turn his life over to God.

But this wasn't the end of his conversion. Three years later, the young man was ordained a priest, the next step in his journey of faith. Then, while vacationing with four other priests on the Amalfi Coast, a sudden storm forced them to shore and they took refuge in a hermitage called St. Mary's of the Mountain. Alphonsus was overwhelmed with the poverty of the townspeople and dedicated himself to serving the poor of the country district. The death of his friend and teacher, Bishop Falcoia, led Alphonsus to take on the role of leader.

The process of conversion continued throughout St. Alphonsus Liguori's life. It's the same for us. God calls us to use our gifts and talents to bring love and truth to our world, and we'll be offered many opportunities for grace and continued conversion.

- *How is God calling you to conversion in your everyday life?*
- *What can you add to your life to continue growing closer to God?*

Conversion Happens Every Day

"Then [Jesus] told them a parable about the necessity for them to pray always without becoming weary."

Luke 18:1

Conversion is a process that takes place every day. Your initial conversion has already taken place. Now it's up to you to make sure the process doesn't stop. Luckily, the Church has given you the tools you need to keep going.

You've learned a lot about prayer during your RCIA sessions. Now it's up to you to use what you've learned. You may not be able to make time for Mass every day (although it's worth trying!). But that doesn't mean you don't have time for any prayer at all. You can offer up a quick prayer for patience when you feel frustrated or thanksgiving when something good happens. You can sacrifice something simple, like listening to music in the car to fit in a decade of the rosary or just some quiet time talking to God in your own words.

"'Pray constantly' (1 Thessalonians 5:17). It is always possible to pray. It is even a vital necessity. Prayer and Christian life are inseparable."

CCC 2757

You can also foster conversion by getting involved in the work of your faith community. We serve the people of God when we become active in parish choirs or music ensembles or when we become lectors or greeters.

"As the work of Christ liturgy is also an action of his Church. It makes the Church present and manifests her as the visible sign of the communion in Christ between God and men. It engages the faithful in the new life of the community and involves the 'conscious, active, and fruitful participation' of everyone."

CCC 1071

You also have unique gifts that enable you to serve your community. If you excel at sports, you might become a coach for a community team. If you have a passion for sharing what you know, you can volunteer your time as a tutor. If you feel called to be the hands of Christ, you could volunteer in a soup kitchen. There are limitless possibilities to share your new faith and the love of Christ in your community.

"What good is it, my brothers, if someone says he has faith but does not have works? Can that faith save him? If a brother or sister has nothing to wear and has no food for the day, and one of you says to them, 'Go in peace, keep warm, and eat well,' but you do not give them the necessities of the body, what good is it? So also faith of itself, if it does not have works, is dead."

James 2:14–17

- *What would happen to your faith if you stopped all faith-related activities after receiving the sacraments of initiation?*
- *What would happen if everyone went out and lived faith as vibrantly and publicly as Jesus did?*

I Thought I'd Have It All Figured Out

Still have questions about your new faith? Welcome to the club! It's nearly impossible for any thinking, active Catholic to go through life without any questions about his or her faith. It's part of the conversion process. Jesus didn't kick out his apostles when they had questions or doubts. He taught them.

Having faith means not knowing with certainty but still believing. Having a relationship with God and the Church means having somewhere to turn with our questions. We might not always get the answers we expect or want, we might not get the answers society tells us are correct, but we're not alone.

"Have you come to believe because you have seen me? Blessed are those who have not seen and have believed."

John 20:29

Conversion Happens Every Day

- As a group, discuss the reflection question, *What would happen to your faith if you stopped all faith related activities after receiving the sacraments of initiation?* Ask participants why they think it's important for all Catholics, not just neophytes, to actively live their faith every day.

I Thought I'd Have it All Figured Out

- Emphasize that the process of conversion contains highs and lows. Periods of doubt are normal, and can be an important part of spiritual growth. Encourage participants not to give up when they have doubts or questions but to seek answers from trusted spiritual mentors.

With a partner or as a group, create a list of things you can do when you have questions about your faith. Be as specific as possible and save this list somewhere you can go back to it.

Suggested responses include: Getting answers from Catholic books, a spiritual director or faithful Catholic, praying about the question, reading Scripture, receiving the sacraments and praying over the question, etc.

With a partner or as a group, create a list of things you can do when you have questions about your faith. Be as specific as possible and save this list where you can go back to it.

What about the ongoing conversion process sounds exciting to you? Why? What sounds scary or intimidating? Why?

Journey of Faith for Teens: Mystagogy, M1 (826320)
Imprimi Potest: Stephen T. Rehrauer, CSsR, Provincial, Denver Province, the Redemptorists.
Imprimatur: "In accordance with CIC 827, permission to publish has been granted on July 12, 2016, by the Rev. Msgr. Mark S. Rivituso, Vicar General, Archdiocese of St. Louis. Permission to publish is an indication that nothing contrary to Church teaching is contained in this work. It does not imply any endorsement of the opinions expressed in the publication; nor is any liability assumed by this permission."
Journey of Faith for Teens © 2000, 2016 Liguori Publications, Liguori, MO 63057. All rights reserved. No part of this publication may be reproduced, distributed, stored, transmitted, or posted in any form by any means without prior written permission. To order, visit Liguori.org or call 800-325-9521. Liguori Publications, a nonprofit corporation, is an apostolate of the Redemptorists. To learn more about the Redemptorists, visit Redemptorists.com.
Editors of 2016 edition: Theresa Nienaber and Pat Fosarelli, MD, DMin. Design: Lorena Mitre Jimenez. Images: Shutterstock.
Scripture texts in this work are taken from the *New American Bible,* revised edition © 2010, 1991, 1986, 1970 Confraternity of Christian Doctrine, Washington, D.C., and are used by permission of the copyright owner. All Rights Reserved. No part of the *New American Bible* may be reproduced in any form without permission in writing from the copyright owner. Excerpts from English translation of the *Catechism of the Catholic Church* for the United States of America © 1994 United States Catholic Conference, Inc.—Libreria Editrice Vaticana; English translation of the *Catechism of the Catholic Church: Modifications from the Editio Typica* © 1997 United States Catholic Conference, Inc.—Libreria Editrice Vaticana. Compliant with *The Roman Missal, Third Edition.*
Printed in the United States of America. 20 19 18 17 16 / 5 4 3 2 1. Third Edition.

ISBN 978-0-7648-2632-0

Liguori
PUBLICATIONS
A Redemptorist Ministry

Journal

What about the ongoing conversion process sounds exciting to you? Why? What sounds scary or intimidating? Why?

Closing Prayer

Listen to the recording of the Easter song you chose for this session. If you aren't able to have music this session, join hands and pray the Lord's Prayer.

Looking Ahead

Before the next session, ask participants to think about how they, as current members of the laity, can serve the Church.

M2: The Role of the Laity

Catechism: 864, 897–913, 940–943, 1546–47, 2442

Objectives

- Recognize that the lay faithful are essential to the life of the Church.

- Identify the ways laypeople live out their call to holiness in the world of family, work, and community.

- Recall that the laity serve the kingdom of God with the ordained and consecrated religious.

Leader Meditation

1 Corinthians 12:12–26

Meditate on the reality that you are an indispensable member of the body of Christ. In what ways do you make the body of Christ more whole and more perfect? In what ways are the young people you teach also indispensable members of Christ's body? How does the Church benefit from the great diversity of its membership?

Leader Preparation

- Read the lesson, this lesson plan, the Scripture passage, and the Catechism sections.

- Invite your parish youth minister (or another knowledgeable parishioner) to attend this session and talk about parish ministry and service opportunities available to young people.

- Find a recording of an Easter song to use for the closing prayer.

- Be familiar with the vocabulary terms for this lesson: common priesthood of the faithful, universal vocation, particular vocation. Definitions are provided in this guide's glossary.

Welcome

Greet neophytes as they arrive. Check for supplies and immediate needs. Solicit questions or comments about the previous sessions and/or share new information and findings. Begin promptly.

Opening Scripture

1 Corinthians 12:12–26

Ask a volunteer to light the candle and read aloud. Ask each participant to look around the room, reflecting silently on how each person in the room brings something unique and important to the body of Christ. Before beginning your discussion of the lesson handout, ask participants to think about **what they bring to the body of Christ**.

> "The very differences which the Lord has willed to put between the members of his body serve its unity and mission. For 'in the Church there is diversity of ministry but unity of mission.'"
>
> *CCC 873*

Journey of Faith

In Short:

- The lay faithful are essential in the life of the Church.

- The laity serve the kingdom of God together with the ordained priesthood and consecrated religious.

- Laypeople live out their call to holiness in the world of family, work, and community.

The Role of the Laity

The members of a parish liturgy planning committee were choosing songs for upcoming Sunday Masses. After deciding on mostly traditional hymns, one liturgist suggested dedicating one Mass time specifically for young adults. "After all," she said, "they're the future of the Church. It's important we have a Mass where they feel welcomed."

That's when a young priest at the table spoke up, "It's important for everyone to feel welcomed at all our Mass times. We're all part of the same Church, no matter what stage or state of life we're in."

- *What do you think the priest meant by his comment?*

- *How can you help others feel welcomed in your parish church?*

Each of us is tremendously important to God's plan for the world. Drawing on the graces received at baptism, members of the **common priesthood of the faithful** serve God's kingdom. God marks all Christians as his children, empowering us to act in Christ's name as priests, prophets, and kings.

"But you are 'a chosen race, a royal priesthood, a holy nation, a people of his own, so that you may announce the praises' of him who called you out of darkness into his wonderful light."

1 Peter 2:9

As *priests*, laypeople offer worship to God, especially by participating in the eucharistic liturgy. As *prophets*, we speak the word of God and witness to the life, teachings, and saving actions of Christ. As *kings*, we profit from the authority and power of God to continue Christ's ministry of service and love to all people.

While never the true definition of the laity, the term layperson once had the connotation of being the passive recipient of the faith. While the ordained priesthood and those in consecrated life were viewed as having the active role of dispensing and passing on the faith. In today's Church, the laity is expected to be anything but passive in their faith.

As a layperson, you're an adopted child of God, a brother or sister of Jesus, and an heir to God's wealth of grace and life eternal, called to serve God's kingdom here on earth.

CCC 864, 897–913, 940–943, 1546–47, 2442

- Set aside time here to allow any guest speakers you've invited to talk about the ways participants can get involved in their parish. At the end of their presentation, give participants time to ask questions and respond to the reflection question. If you aren't able to get a guest speaker, you can briefly mention ways young people can get involved in your parish and then give participants time for the reflection.

The Role of the Laity

- Read the introduction section together, then ask participants for their initial reaction to this conversation. Have they ever felt unwelcome or isolated because of their age?

- Discuss the state of life participants are currently in and ask what the challenges and opportunities of this state are. If you have any stories about how you felt about your faith or parish when you were a teen, share along with the group.

- Discuss the two reflection questions as a group.

- Read 1 Peter 2:9 to the group out loud. Ask participants what they believe the sacred author meant when he referred to us as "a chosen race, a royal priesthood, a holy nation."

Suggested responses include: We are set apart for God, we are called to the priesthood of the faithful, we are God's chosen people, we belong to God first and the world second, etc.

A Shared Work

- Ask participants what they think it means to live counterculturally. Then discuss what it means to live counterculturally as a Christian.

- Emphasize that we all have opportunities to serve in our everyday lives at home or at school. Our ministry isn't just limited to volunteer work or the parish youth group.

Doing God's Work in the World

- Discuss the difference between universal vocation and particular vocation.

- Discuss how we can live out our universal vocation and our particular vocation and how these two calls may overlap.

- As teen participants are likely still discerning their particular vocation, ask how living out our universal vocation might make it easier to discover our particular vocation.

- Give participants time to answer the reflection questions.

"No part of the structure of a living body is merely passive but has a share in the functions as well as life of the body: so, too, in the body of Christ, which is the Church."

Decree on the Apostolate of the Laity (Apostolicam Actuositatem), 2

- *How do you feel called to be active in your faith life? The faith life of your parish? The Church?*

A Shared Work

Though the ordained priesthood is unique, bishops, priests, and deacons work in collaboration with the laity. Christ sends the laity into the world to transform the values of society and individuals into those of the kingdom of God, to minister as he would minister. This means we are sometimes called to act counterculturally, to go against what may be expected in secular culture and act as Jesus would.

Before his passion and death, Christ prayed for all his disciples, present and future:

"They do not belong to the world any more than I belong to the world. Consecrate them in the truth. Your word is truth. As you sent me into the world, so I sent them into the world."

John 17:16–18

As laypeople, we go into the world "bearing consistent witness in [our] personal, family, and social lives by proclaiming and sharing the gospel of Christ in every situation in which [we] find [our]selves" (*On Certain Questions Regarding the Collaboration of the Non-ordained Faithful in the Sacred Ministry of the Priest*).

- *What do you think it means to live counterculturally, like Jesus?*

- *How do you already minister as Jesus would in your life?*

Doing God's Work in the World

That call to holiness and living a life like Jesus is our **universal vocation**, the vocation we are all called to live. Each of us also has a **particular vocation**, that is, we are called to a vocation that is specific to each of us. The priesthood of the faithful includes celibate religious, married, and single persons. All of these vocations comes with special gifts and opportunities to serve.

"Love is...the fundamental and innate vocation of every human being.... Christian revelation recognizes two specific ways of realizing the vocation of the human person in its entirety, to love: marriage and virginity or celibacy. Either one is, in its own proper form, an actuation of the most profound truth of man, of his being 'created in the image of God.'"

Pope St. John Paul II, On the Role of the Christian Family in the Modern World (Familiaris Consortio), 11

- *How are you currently living out your universal vocation?*

- *Have you felt God calling you to a particular vocation?*

As Married Couples and Parents

Husbands and wives are called to help their spouse and children along the path to sainthood. Their primary responsibilities revolve around their family, their domestic church. Other kinds of service in the Church follow after these primary responsibilities.

"Thus the home is the first school of Christian life and 'a school for human enrichment.' Here one learns endurance and the joy of work, fraternal love, generous—even repeated—forgiveness, and above all divine worship in prayer and the offering of one's life."

CCC 1657

As Single Adults

While being single is considered a state of life, not a primary vocation like marriage, priesthood, and consecrated life, we all share in the fundamental call of Christians to love. Belonging to God and our call to holiness extends to all states of life. Those living in the single state of life may or may not be called to a lifetime of being single, but can use their single state to devote more time to serving others and being engaged in the community.

Scripture gives us many models for how to live our universal vocation in the single state of life. Jesus was single, as were Mary, Martha, Lazarus, and others. Saint Paul saw much value in the single state and encouraged others to use their gifts within the single life:

"Each has a particular gift from God, one of one kind and one of another. Now to the unmarried and to widows I say: it is a good thing for them to remain as they are, as I do."

1 Corinthians 7:7–8

As Workers

Whether you have a part-time job or are a full-time student, the work you do every day is an opportunity to glorify God. The way we do our chores, the effort we put into our schoolwork, how we treat those we meet during the day can all be powerful ways to witness to the grace of God.

"Let the word of Christ dwell in you richly, as in all wisdom you teach and admonish one another, singing psalms, hymns, and spiritual songs with gratitude in your hearts to God. And whatever you do, in word or in deed, do everything in the name of the Lord Jesus, giving thanks to God the Father through him."

Colossians 3:16–17

- How might someone see the Catholic Church after meeting you?
- How can you strengthen the connection between your faith and your life?

As Church Members

Some laypeople are called to perform tasks that assist priests in serving the needs of the community by ministries such as service to shut-ins. Some use their gifts in parish or diocesan administration, pastoral ministry, chaplaincy, bereavement ministry, or faith formation. Others participate in liturgical ministries such as lector, cantor, or extraordinary minister of holy Communion.

"There are innumerable opportunities open to the laity for the exercise of their apostolate of evangelization and sanctification."

Decree on the Apostolate of the Laity
(Apostolicam Actuositatem), 6

As Community Members and Citizens

Finally, the laity touches the lives of friends, extended family, and community in unique and deeply personal ways.

"Religion that is pure and undefiled before God and the Father is this: to care for orphans and widows in their affliction and to keep oneself unstained by the world."

James 1:27

Getting Ready, Getting Involved

As you become more mature in your faith you may have questions or be asked questions about your faith that you don't know the answers to right now. That's why it's important that your faith formation never ends. Stay involved in your local parish or Catholic campus ministry and look for opportunities to receive the sacraments of Eucharist and reconciliation often, as well as opportunities for ongoing faith formation, social outreach, and community involvement.

You can also continue to grow your faith on your own through regular prayer, studying Scripture, and reading good books about faith topics of interest or the spiritual lives of holy people you admire.

As Workers

- Give participants time to answer the reflection questions on their own, then ask for volunteers to share.

- As a group, create a list of all the ways participants hope others see the Catholic Church after meeting them. Then discuss how participants can share those characteristics of the Church to everyone they meet in obvious and subtle ways.

On your own or with a partner, write a prayer asking God to help young Christians live out their universal vocation. Share this prayer with the rest of the group at the end of the session.

On your own or with a partner, write a prayer asking God to help young Christians live out their universal vocation. Share this prayer with the rest of the group at the end of the session.

What parish or community ministries do you feel called to participate in? How can you get started?

Journey of Faith for Teens: Mystagogy, M2 (826320)
Imprimi Potest: Stephen T. Rehrauer, CSsR, Provincial, Denver Province, the Redemptorists.
Imprimatur: "In accordance with CIC 827, permission to publish has been granted on July 12, 2016, by the Rev. Msgr. Mark S. Rivituso, Vicar General, Archdiocese of St. Louis. Permission to publish is an indication that nothing contrary to Church teaching is contained in this work. It does not imply any endorsement of the opinions expressed in the publication; nor is any liability assumed by this permission."
Journey of Faith for Teens © 2000, 2016 Liguori Publications, Liguori, MO 63057. All rights reserved. No part of this publication may be reproduced, distributed, stored, transmitted, or posted in any form by any means without prior written permission. To order, visit Liguori.org or call 800-325-9521. Liguori Publications, a nonprofit corporation, is an apostolate of the Redemptorists. To learn more about the Redemptorists, visit Redemptorists.com. Editors of 2016 edition: Theresa Nienaber and Pat Fosarelli, MD, DMin. Design: Lorena Mitre Jimenez. Images: Shutterstock.
Scripture texts in this work are taken from the *New American Bible*, revised edition © 2010, 1991, 1986, 1970 Confraternity of Christian Doctrine, Washington, D.C., and are used by permission of the copyright owner. All Rights Reserved. No part of the *New American Bible* may be reproduced in any form without permission in writing from the copyright owner. Excerpts from English translation of the *Catechism of the Catholic Church* for the United States of America © 1994 United States Catholic Conference, Inc.—*Libreria Editrice Vaticana;* English translation of the *Catechism of the Catholic Church:* Modifications from the *Editio Typica* © 1997 United States Catholic Conference, Inc.—*Libreria Editrice Vaticana.* Compliant with *The Roman Missal, Third Edition.*
Printed in the United States of America. 20 19 18 17 16 / 5 4 3 2 1. Third Edition.

Liguori
PUBLICATIONS
A Redemptorist Ministry

Journal

What parish or community ministries do you feel called to participate in? How can you get started?

Closing Prayer

Go around the group and ask participants to share the prayers they wrote in the activity section. Then play the song you chose for today's closing prayer.

Take Home

Encourage participants to call or email the coordinator of a parish ministry they'd like to get involved in.

M3: Your Spiritual Gifts

Catechism: 797–810, 2690

Objectives

- List the seven gifts of the Holy Spirit named in 1 Corinthians 12.

- Recognize that all spiritual gifts are to be used out of love and in service to others.

- Have participants discern the gifts in their own lives, and how to use them for the Church and their community.

Leader Meditation

1 Corinthians 12:4–11

Saint Paul tells us that "there are different ministries but the same Lord." Think about your important ministry as a catechist to young people. What special gifts related to this work has the Spirit given you? Bring them to mind and offer a prayer of thanksgiving. Know that the Church is grateful for the way you share your gifts.

Leader Preparation

- Read the lesson, this lesson plan, the Scripture passage, and the *Catechism* sections.

- Find a recording of an Easter song to use for the closing prayer.

- Have extra copies of the Bible and *Catechism*.

Welcome

Greet neophytes as they arrive. Check for supplies and immediate needs. Solicit questions or comments about the previous sessions and/or share new information and findings. Begin promptly.

Opening Scripture

1 Corinthians 12:4–11

Ask a volunteer to light the candle and read aloud. Before beginning your discussion of the lesson handout, **ask participants to consider which gifts mentioned in this passage they have been given for the building up of the body of Christ**.

"The Holy Spirit is 'the principle of every vital and truly saving action in each part of the Body.' He works in many ways to build up the whole body in charity."

CCC 798

In Short:

- Various gifts of the Holy Spirit can be discovered in the lives of the faithful.
- All spiritual gifts are to be used out of love for and in service to one another.
- We're each responsible for discerning, developing, and sharing our spiritual gifts.

Your Spiritual Gifts

"There are different kinds of spiritual gifts but the same Spirit; there are different forms of service but the same Lord; there are different' workings but the same God who produces all of them in everyone. To each individual the manifestation of the Spirit is given for some benefit. To one is given through the Spirit the expression of wisdom; to another the expression of knowledge according to the same Spirit; to another faith by the same Spirit; to another gifts of healing by the one Spirit; to another mighty deeds; to another prophecy; to another discernment of spirits; to another varieties of tongues; to another interpretation of tongues. But one and the same Spirit produces all of these, distributing them individually to each person as he wishes."

1 Corinthians 12:4–11

You can't picture yourself as a prophet or performing mighty deeds? You're not a straight-A student or an all-star athlete? You don't think you have any special gifts? You think the Holy Spirit just passed right over you?

The Holy Spirit didn't leave you out. We all receive our spiritual gifts through baptism, gifts that we're called to use to unify the body of Christ and to help spread the message of God's kingdom. You didn't get to choose your spiritual gifts, God bestows them on us through the work of the Holy Spirit, but you are called to use them out of love for an in service to others.

"So that she can fulfill her mission, the Holy Spirit 'bestows upon [the Church] varied hierarchic and charismatic gifts, and in this way directs her.' 'Henceforward the Church, endowed with the gifts of her founder and faithfully observing his precepts of charity, humility and self-denial, receives the mission of proclaiming and establishing among all peoples the Kingdom of Christ and of God, and she is on earth the seed and the beginning of that kingdom.'"

CCC 768; citing Dogmatic Constitution on the Church (Lumen Gentium), 4–5

But before you fully appreciate or make use of your gifts from the Holy Spirit, you have to open them and fully appreciate what you've been given. Once you've discerned and understand your gifts, you'll be better equipped to share them within your community and beyond.

CCC 797–810, 2690

Your Spiritual Gifts

- Depending on your time for this session and your personal preference, you can read through each of the gifts of the Spirit as a group or you can divide participants up into seven groups and make each of them responsible for teaching the rest of the group about their assigned gift. If you decide on groups, make sure you have copies of the *Catechism* and Bibles to share so groups can do more research than just reading the lesson handout.

The Gift of Wisdom

- For each of the bullets listed, ask participants to think of a scenario in which someone responds or reacts with wisdom.

Suggested responses include: Your friend comes to you with questions about how science and religion can coexist. instead of arguing, you invite the friend to join a small group at your parish that discusses this topic, etc.

- As a group, respond to the reflection question, *What other actions or ministries require the gift of wisdom?*

Suggested responses include: Evangelizing to others, responding to questions about the faith, knowing when it's better not to respond (out of anger or resentment), etc.

The Gift of Knowledge

- For each of the bullets listed, ask participants to think of a scenario in which someone responds or reacts with knowledge.

Suggested responses include: After years of music lessons you volunteer to teach beginning music after school to elementary students just starting out, etc.

- As a group, respond to the reflection question, *What other actions or ministries require the gift of knowledge?*

Suggested responses include: All those who teach the faith to others like catechists or spiritual directors, priests require it to preach, etc.

The Gift of Faith

- For each of the bullets listed, ask participants to think of a scenario in which someone responds or reacts with faith.

Suggested responses include: When given the opportunity to do volunteer work you step outside your comfort zone to work with the homeless because it's where you feel called instead of working where you feel more comfortable, etc.

- As a group, respond to the reflection question, *What other actions or ministries require the gift of faith?*

Suggested responses include: Leaving home to be a missionary, continuing to search for answers when you have doubts, joining the consecrated or religious life, etc.

The Gift of Healing

- For each of the bullets listed, ask participants to think of a scenario in which someone responds or reacts with healing.

Suggested responses include: You know your grandma has always gone to Mass on Sundays, but now that she can't drive she's worried she won't be able to go. So you volunteer to pick her up and take her home every week, etc.

- As a group, respond to the reflection question, *What other actions or ministries require the gift of healing?*

MYSTAGOGY

JOURNEY OF FAITH

The Gift of Wisdom

"Who among you is wise and understanding? Let him show his works by a good life in the humility that comes from wisdom."

James 3:13

It's said that wisdom comes with age, but it's not automatic. Wisdom is a gift of the Holy Spirit that's attained through having an open mind, learning from experience, knowing human nature, and knowing that God is alive and active in our world. It changes the way we live.

We use the gift of wisdom when we:

- Informally counsel others.
- Discourage harmful or destructive behavior in our friends.
- Participate in small faith groups.

- What other actions or ministries require the gift of wisdom?

The Gift of Knowledge

"The heart of the intelligent acquires knowledge, and the ear of the wise seeks knowledge."

Proverbs 18:15

We all have knowledge we can share with others. The important thing isn't how much knowledge we have, but how we use it. Our goal shouldn't be to use our knowledge to prove other people wrong or to prove how smart we are. We should use our knowledge for the benefit of others.

We use the gift of knowledge when we:

- Volunteer as after-school tutors for students in need of extra help.
- Help a younger sibling with a science project, scouting event, etc.
- Assist coaches who manage teams for younger athletes.

- What other actions or ministries require the gift of knowledge?

The Gift of Faith

"[I]f you have faith the size of a mustard seed, you will say to this mountain, 'Move from here to there,' and it will move. Nothing will be impossible for you."

Matthew 17:20

The gift of faith is easy to take for granted. But Jesus told us we can move mountains with the true gift of faith. Faith gives us the ability to hope even while we're suffering.

We use the gift of faith when we:

- Pray, as individuals or as members of a group.
- Work in a food pantry, homeless shelter, or crisis pregnancy center.
- Offer sincere words of hope or encouragement to someone who is sad.

- What other actions or ministries require the gift of faith?

The Gift of Healing

"Cure the sick, raise the dead, cleanse lepers, drive out demons. Without cost you have received; without cost you are to give."

Matthew 10:8

When we think of healing, we may think of miraculous return to physical health that defies explanation. But while healing does sometimes include a miraculous cure, healing doesn't always mean restoring physical health. Healing takes place in the spirit as well as in the body. Any time we help lift a depressed spirit, bring a smile, or touch a hurting heart, we are using our gift of healing.

We use the gift of healing when we:

- Drive those in nursing homes to Mass.
- Spend time with the homebound.
- Bring assignments to sick classmates.

> • *What other actions or ministries require the gift of healing?*

The Gift of Working Mighty Deeds

"[Jesus] noticed a poor widow putting in two small coins. He said, "I tell you truly, this poor widow put in more than all the rest; for those others have all made offerings from their surplus wealth, but she, from her poverty, has offered her whole livelihood."

Luke 21:2–4

Putting in only two small coins doesn't sound like a mighty deed, but behind this small act was a mighty sacrifice and required mighty faith in God. The mighty deeds of the Holy Spirit aren't necessarily big in the eyes of the world. Sometimes these deeds are small acts done with great love and trust in God; the humble, thoughtful services that no one else will do.

We use the gift of working mighty deeds when we:

- Serve refreshments at parish functions.
- Clean or maintaining our church, school, or home.
- Do yard work or chores for the elderly.

> • *What other actions or ministries require the gift of working mighty deeds?*

The Gift of Prophecy

"No prophecy ever came through human will; but rather human beings moved by the holy Spirit spoke under the influence of God."

2 Peter 1:21

Prophecy for the Christian is not foretelling the future. Prophecy is living according to God's values and announcing them in situations where they don't appear to be present. When you have the courage to stand up for injustice or to speak out in defense of a bullied classmate you are using the gift of prophecy. Sometimes prophets make statements that don't agree with popular opinion, and that's why Christian prophecy requires a great deal of courage and trust in God.

We use the gift of prophecy when we:

- Join a parish social-justice group.
- Help make our parish and school welcoming for all.
- Speak out when our friends act in ways that oppose a Christian lifestyle.

> • *What other actions or ministries require the gift of prophecy?*

The Gift of Discernment of Spirits

"My son, if you receive my words and treasure my commands, Turning your ear to wisdom, inclining your heart to understanding; Yes, if you call for intelligence, and to understanding raise your voice...Then will you understand the fear of the LORD; the knowledge of God you will find."

Proverbs 2:1-5

It's easy to write off people we think are hostile, critical, or simply don't agree with us. Discernment of spirits means that instead of writing people off based on our first, human impression, we look at them and the situation the way God would. When we reflect on a situation to determine and understand what God would want us to do, we are using the gift of discernment of spirits.

We need the gift of discernment of spirits when we:

- Serve on student council or take on a leadership role in our parish youth group.
- Mediate differences among our friends.
- Organize or seek out volunteers for service projects.

The Gift of Prophecy

- For each of the bullets listed, ask participants to think of a scenario in which someone responds or reacts with the gift of prophecy.

Suggested responses include: You notice someone your age who always goes to Mass alone, the next time you see the person, you ask him or her to sit with you, and at the end of Mass invite her or him to join your parish youth group, etc.

- As a group, respond to the reflection question, *What other actions or ministries require the gift of prophecy?*

Suggested responses include: Speaking out when you see actions that go against the dignity of the person, participating in pro-life rallies or marches, vocalizing the Catholic perspective in class debates, etc.

The Gift of Discernment of Spirits

- For each of the bullets listed, ask participants to think of a scenario in which someone responds or reacts with discernment of spirits.

Suggested responses include: You know one of your friends has a beautiful voice, so you suggest she cantor at Mass and agree to be there to support her for her "debut," etc.

- As a group, respond to the reflection question, *What other actions or ministries require the gift of discernment of spirits?*

Suggested responses include: Making an effort to get to know people and their interests or talents, taking the time to understanding the perspectives of people we disagree with, etc.

M3

Suggested responses include: Volunteering to work in a hospital or rehab center, offering encouragement to a distressed friend, making yourself available to a classmate who needs to talk and really listening, etc.

The Gift of Working Mighty Deeds

- For each of the bullets listed, ask participants to think of a scenario in which someone responds or reacts by working mighty deeds.

Suggested responses include: You notice your elderly neighbor hasn't been able to rake their leaves yet this fall, even though they've always been meticulous about their yard in the past. So you rake your neighbor's yard at the same time your family is working on your yard, etc.

- As a group, respond to the reflection question, *What other actions or ministries require the gift of working mighty deeds?*

Suggested responses include: Responding kindly when someone is rude to you, picking up trash in the hallway between classes, volunteering to do chores at home before you're asked, etc.

The Gift of Tongues

- For each of the bullets listed, ask participants to think of a scenario in which someone responds or reacts with the gift of tongues.

Suggested responses include: The lectors at your parish are all older, and you want to see more young people represented as participating in the Mass, too, so you volunteer to be a lector and a role model for younger parishioners, etc.

- As a group, respond to the reflection question, *What other actions or ministries require the gift of tongues?*

Suggested responses include: Evangelizing to people where they are in their faith and not talking down to them, voicing compliments instead of just thinking them, etc.

The Gift of Interpreting Tongues

- For each of the bullets listed, ask participants to think of a scenario in which someone responds or reacts with the gift of interpreting tongues.

Suggested responses include: Your dad has been more critical than normal and it seems like all you do is yell at each other. You know there must be something else going on, so before you get into another argument you ask if there's anything you can do to help out, etc.

- As a group, respond to the reflection question, *What other actions or ministries require the gift of interpreting tongues?*

Suggested responses include: Responding to criticism with compassion, responding to others with empathy, offering to help family members or friends who seem overwhelmed, etc.

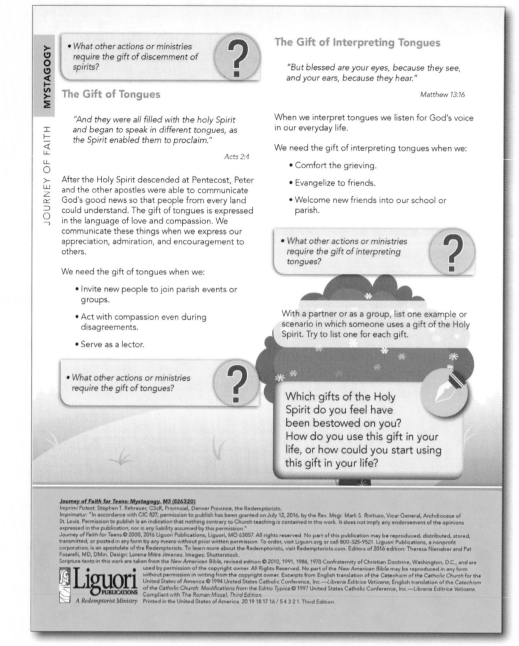

With a partner or as a group, list one example or scenario in which someone uses a gift of the Holy Spirit. Try to list one for each gift.

Journaling

Which gifts of the Holy Spirit do you feel have been especially bestowed on you? How do you use this gift in your life, or how could you start using this gift in your life?

Closing Prayer

Conclude with the song you've chosen for today's session or, if you are unable to play music, pray the Lord's Prayer as a group.

Looking Ahead

The gifts of the Holy Spirit are meant to help us as we go about the work God has planned for us to do. Ask participants to think about how their gifts may be preparing them for a specific ministry.

M4: Discernment

Catechism: 407, 800, 1776–94

Objectives

- Define spiritual discernment as a decision-making process in which one seeks God's will.

- Follow the seven steps of St. Ignatius of Loyola's discernment process.

- Recognize that discernment plays a large part in our spiritual growth and faith journey.

Leader Meditation

Hebrews 13:7, 16–21

Though St. Paul is confident that he has a clear conscience, he realizes that he will also need the guidance of the Holy Spirit through prayer. He is describing the process of discernment. Spend a moment considering the ways you presently make difficult decisions. Do you practice discernment?

Leader Preparation

- Read the lesson, this lesson plan, the Scripture passage, and the *Catechism* sections.

- Find a recording of an Easter song to use for the closing prayer.

- Be familiar with the vocabulary terms for this lesson: discernment, inner freedom. Definitions are provided in this guide's glossary.

Welcome

Greet neophytes as they arrive. Check for supplies and immediate needs. Solicit questions or comments about the previous sessions and/or share new information and findings. Begin promptly.

Opening Scripture

Hebrews 13:7, 16–21

Ask a volunteer to light the candle and read out loud. Before beginning your discussion of the lesson handout, ask participants to reflect on **the need for God's input in our decision making**.

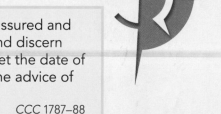

"Man is sometimes confronted by situations that make moral judgments less assured and decisions difficult. But he must always seriously seek what is right and good and discern the will of God expressed in divine law. To this purpose, man strives to interpret the date of experience and the signs of the times assisted by the virtue of prudence, by the advice of competent people, and by the help of the Holy Spirit and his gifts."

CCC 1787–88

Journey of Faith

In Short:

- Spiritual discernment is a decision-making process in which we seek God's will.
- Saint Ignatius of Loyola offers a seven-step discernment process.
- Discernment plays a large part in our spiritual growth and faith journey.

Discernment

Did I pick the right college major? Should I get more involved with youth group? Do I quit my part-time job to make more time for volunteer work?

Life is full of decisions, and a lot of us would like to be able to just ask God what we need to do and have God give us the right answer. It can be difficult to know what God is calling us to do with our lives, especially when it seems like everything in our lives is changing all at once or when we don't have much time left to make a choice.

- How do you make big decisions?
- Do you tend to follow your head or your heart?

While God might not send us a timeline of exactly what we need to live out his plan for us, we can still get divine guidance as we make decisions. As Christians, we believe that the Holy Spirit lives within us and gives us a sense of God's will for our lives. Before Jesus left this world, he promised us the gift of his Spirit, telling his disciples:

"I will ask the Father, and he will give you another Advocate to be with you always, the Spirit of truth, which the world cannot accept, because it neither sees nor knows it. But you know it, because it remains with you, and will be in you."

John 14:16–17

The Holy Spirit leads us into the truth and helps us discover and walk God's path for our lives. But the Holy Spirit isn't the only voice that seeks to guide us. There are many other voices in the world competing for our attention and trying to influence us in a particular direction—and not all of these voices have our best interest in mind.

- What other voices try to influence your decisions?
- Which of these voices are positive influences? Why?
- Which voices are influences you try to avoid? Why?

CCC 407, 800, 1776–94

Discernment

- Give participants time to answer the first two reflection questions on their own.

- Discuss common decision-making processes as a group. If you have somewhere to write down this list, like a white board or smart board, do so, otherwise encourage participants to take notes. Emphasize the ways we come to a decision and how certain processes work better for some people than others.

- As a group, answer the next three reflection questions. If you've been making a list somewhere, add these factors to it.

Suggested responses include: Our parents, friends, and even cultural forces like the media may try to influence us; those who have our best interest at heart are positive influences (usually our parents, true friends, mentors, or teachers); the influences to avoid are those who want us to act against our conscience and in ways we know aren't Christian.

- Emphasize that while most of us have a well-formed conscience, it's still important that we allow the guidance of the Holy Spirit into our lives to keep it that way. The Holy Spirit is our advocate and the spirit of truth. It is the one voice that will *always* lead us closer to God.

Seven Steps of Discernment

- The seven steps of discernment are sometimes easier to understand when applied to an actual dilemma. You may choose to simply go through each step with the group or use a hypothetical dilemma to walk through each step as a group together. If you have extra time, you could also divide participants into small groups, have them pick a different dilemma to use the steps of discernment on, and then present to the whole group on their conclusion.

- An example is included below. You may use this with your class or make up your own.

1. You are trying to determine if you should end a friendship with someone who has become a bad influence.

2. You could stay in the friendship and hope that you could guide your friend toward better choices. But you are worried that you're going to get dragged into these bad decisions before you could make a difference. To gather information you could: talk to your friend about your concerns and explain the dilemma you're in (which would be uncomfortable, might lead to a fight, and could end in you losing that friendship anyway); talk to your parents or trusted adult mentor about how you can handle this situation; if your friend is in danger or could cause harm to someone else you could let your friend's parents and other adult authority figure know what's going on (you may lose your friend's trust, but at least you know your friend will be safe).

The process of making a well-informed, thoughtful decision is called discernment. Authentic discernment can be complicated because of our lack of self-knowledge and our desire for God to say "yes" to what we want, which can lead to us manipulating or ignoring the guidance we receive from the Spirit. However, as long as we have a willingness to learn and an openness to the Holy Spirit, we'll begin to notice and discern the true voice of God.

There's no one-size-fits-all path that leads us to God's will with certainty in all situations. It's not that easy. But there are some guidelines that can help you grow in your ability to know and understand God's will when you're faced with a decision. Saint Ignatius of Loyola offers some guidelines in his *Spiritual Exercises* that can get you started. As you grow in faith and cultivate the gift of discernment, you'll develop a method that works best for you. To get you started, below are seven steps based on the guidelines of St. Ignatius of Loyola.

Seven Steps of Discernment

1. State the decision you need to make clearly.

Before you can discern what God is calling you to do, you need to know what you're trying to decide. For example: *Should I end this relationship or friendship? Should I choose this college? Should I get more involved in this form of ministry?* As you focus on this question, be sure to remember God throughout the decision-making process. Continuously ask God for help in knowing his truth and ask God to give you the inner freedom and courage to carry out that truth.

2. Gather important information.

Think about the possible choices you could make. Consider the advantages and disadvantages of each alternative. Be creative as you think about each possible scenario. A situation that may seem to have only two options, like continuing or ending a friendship, may have more possibilities. You might be able to work toward a compromise after a disagreement or only see that friend under certain conditions.

It may help to write down the pros and cons of each alternative. Include the effects of each alternative on your relationship with God, family, the community, or others. Also consider how each alternative may affect your life. Is God calling you to step out of your comfort zone and change the way things have always been? Is God asking you to use your talents in a way you never expected, planned for, or thought of before? Identify any potential obstacles to carrying out each alternative and determine which ones are valid (like, this alternative would put someone else at risk or clearly goes against what you know is right) and which ones only seem to be obstacles (like, fear of the unknown or the desire for things to stay familiar and unchanged).

This process requires a lot of honesty, courage, and patience. If you feel you need a second opinion, ask a trusted friend or advisor who you know has a strong faith and will help you put God's will first.

3. Bring your information to prayer.

The heart of Christian discernment is bringing all our available options to prayer and seeing which option gives us the greatest sense of God's presence, peace, and joy.

As you begin to bring these options to prayer, you may notice there's one option you want more than all the others. If there is, ask yourself: *How am I willing to let go of this option if God calls me in another direction?*

It's easy to get attached to a particular option, and that attachment can keep us from really listening if God calls us somewhere else. That's why we pray for the grace of inner freedom. Inner freedom means that we are free from our emotions and unhealthy attachments and truly open to making a decision centered on what God is calling us to do.

3. In this instance, it may be easier to just hope your influence will rub off on your friend. That keeps you from any uncomfortable conversations, and things can stay the way they are. But is this what God is calling you to do? How would Jesus respond in this situation?

This part of the discernment process is the most important and the most challenging. It isn't easy to sincerely pray, "Thy kingdom come, thy will (not mine) be done." Though if you've prayed for the grace of inner freedom and sincerely desire the Spirit to work in your decision-making process, it can get easier. Our truest self always desires God's will. It's our false, unredeemed self that falls to the temptations of earthly freedom and happiness.

Saint Ignatius suggests three exercises to help us as we consider our decision:

- What advice would you give to someone else facing the same decision?

- Imagine you're on your deathbed looking back over your life. What would you wish to have chosen?

- Imagine standing before God at the Final Judgment. What decision would you wish to have chosen?

4. Make a decision.

At some point we have to make a decision. We go with the option that gives us the most peace in prayer.

But what if none of the options available to you give you any real peace in prayer? In that situation, you can either postpone the decision or choose the one least troublesome option. But if you're having a lot of doubt, and you have time before a decision needs to be made, keep praying and wait to make a decision until you find one that fills you with peace.

God's option may not always be the most attractive one or the choice we desire. Doing the right thing can be painfully difficult, especially when you know it will result in the loss of a friend or letting go of a dream you've held for a long time. However, those initial tears of sadness often turn into tears of joy later on.

5. Live with the decision.

It's a good idea to live with your decision for a while before you move forward with it. This is especially important if you tend to make decisions in the heat of the moment. Ask the Holy Spirit to give you the power and courage to act on what you believe to be God's will for you.

6. Act on the decision.

Actually going through with your decision may seem like an obvious step, but this can be the most difficult. Your decision may involve giving up something you're still hesitant to let go. Keep asking the Holy Spirit for power and courage.

7. Seek confirmation of the decision.

If your choice brings you peace and bears good fruit, you can be sure you are acting in accord with God's will. That doesn't mean there won't be struggles or times you doubt you made the right choice.

Knowing you made a sincere effort to seek God's will is enough. Discernment is something we learn through trial and error, and even with the Holy Spirit as our guide we can wander into bad decisions on our own. God doesn't demand that we always discern perfectly all the time. God asks us only that we actively and sincerely seek his will, act on what we discern, and ask for forgiveness and direction when we realize we've strayed.

4. After prayer, you determine you need to talk to your friend and let your friend know how you feel about certain decisions.

5. You decide to wait a week before sitting down with your friend to have this conversation. What's running through your mind now?

6. You sit down with your friend and actually have the conversation.

7. After your conversation, do you feel like you've done the right thing? Have you done it in the right way? Were you able to be loving and firm in your stance? Does this keep you on a path that leads to a stronger relationship with God?

As a group or with a partner, brainstorm other things you can do to discern God's will when faced with a difficult decision.

As a group or with a partner, brainstorm other things you can do to discern God's will when faced with a difficult decision.

As you went through these seven steps and thought more about discernment, was there a particular decision that kept coming into your mind? Think about that decision and reflect on it. Over the course of the next few days, weeks, or even months, work toward discerning God's will.

Journey of Faith for Teens: Mystagogy, M4 (826320)
Imprimi Potest: Stephen T. Rehrauer, CSsR, Provincial, Denver Province, the Redemptorists.
Imprimatur: "In accordance with CIC 827, permission to publish has been granted on July 12, 2016, by the Rev. Msgr. Mark S. Rivituso, Vicar General, Archdiocese of St. Louis. Permission to publish is an indication that nothing contrary to Church teaching is contained in this work. It does not imply any endorsement of the opinions expressed in the publication; nor is any liability assumed by this permission."
Journey of Faith for Teens © 2000, 2016 Liguori Publications, Liguori, MO 63057. All rights reserved. No part of this publication may be reproduced, distributed, stored, transmitted, or posted in any form by any means without prior written permission. To order, visit Liguori.org or call 800-325-9521. Liguori Publications, a nonprofit corporation, is an apostolate of the Redemptorists. To learn more about the Redemptorists, visit Redemptorists.com. Editors of 2016 edition: Theresa Nienaber and Pat Fosarelli, MD, DMin. Design: Lorena Mitre Jimenez. Images: Shutterstock.
Scripture texts in this work are taken from the *New American Bible*, revised edition © 2010, 1991, 1986, 1970 Confraternity of Christian Doctrine, Washington, D.C., and are used by permission of the copyright owner. All Rights Reserved. No part of the *New American Bible* may be reproduced in any form without permission in writing from the copyright owner. Excerpts from English translation of the *Catechism of the Catholic Church* for the United States of America © 1994 United States Catholic Conference, Inc.—*Libreria Editrice Vaticana*; English translation of the *Catechism of the Catholic Church: Modifications from the Editio Typica* © 1997 United States Catholic Conference, Inc.—*Libreria Editrice Vaticana*. Compliant with *The Roman Missal, Third Edition.*
Printed in the United States of America. 20 19 18 17 16 / 5 4 3 2 1. Third Edition.

Liguori
PUBLICATIONS
A Redemptorist Ministry

Journaling

As you went through these seven steps and thought more about discernment, was there a particular decision that kept coming into your mind? Think about that decision and reflect on it. Over the course of the next few days, weeks, or even months, work toward discerning God's will.

Closing Prayer

Ask participants to think about an important decision that has been weighing on their mind. Have participants offer that decision up to God silently as you pray with the song you've chosen for today's closing prayer. If music is unavailable, pray the Glory Be together.

Take-Home

Ask participants to remember these seven steps when they are faced with an important decision and encourage participants to journal about this decision in their prayer journal.

M5: Our Call to Holiness

Catechism: 2012–16, 1691–98, 2028, 2427

Objectives

- Recognize the significance of the universal call to holiness for Christian living.

- Define holiness as something that happens—usually gradually—with the help of the Holy Spirit.

- Identify obstacles to holiness and actions that grow holiness.

Leader Meditation

1 Peter 1:15–16;
Hebrews 12:14–29

Following Jesus Christ entails becoming like him. We have not been called to an unapproachable kingdom, but an unshakable one—the city of the living God. We have encountered the Holy Mass, where Jesus Christ comes to each of us. We are called to pursue the holiness of Jesus we receive in the Eucharist to become like the one we are receiving. Where are you on this journey to holiness?

Leader Preparation

- Read the lesson, this lesson plan, the Scripture passage, and the *Catechism* sections.

- Find a recording of an Easter song to use for the closing prayer.

- Be familiar with the vocabulary term for this lesson: holiness. The definition is provided in this guide's glossary.

Welcome

Greet neophytes as they arrive. Check for supplies and immediate needs. Solicit questions or comments about the previous sessions and/or share new information and findings. Begin promptly.

Opening Scripture

1 Peter 1:15–16;
Hebrews 12:14–29

Ask for a volunteer to light the candle and read aloud. Discuss as a group the great invitation to receive Jesus Christ in the Holy Mass. Before beginning your discussion of the lesson handout, ask participants **what we learn about holiness from the life of Christ. What changes do we have to make to become more like Christ?**

> "'All Christians in any state or walk of life are called to the fullness of Christian life and to the perfection of charity.' All are called to holiness: 'Be perfect, as your heavenly Father is perfect.'"
>
> CCC 2013

Journey of Faith

In Short:

- All Christians are called to holiness.
- Growth in holiness is a lifelong pursuit.
- We can overcome obstacles to holiness with the Holy Spirit's help.

You've probably heard the expression, "If you want something, you have to work for it." Like Tom in the story above, we work for the things we really want to achieve. We schedule practice time, ask for help from others, and work at it.

When it comes to living a life like Christ, the same principle applies. If we want a life of holiness, we have to work for it. When you think of the word *holy*, you might think of the pope, the saints, your parish priest, your friends who are always at church or doing volunteer work, but you might not think of yourself. You may be thinking holy is an achievable goal for *them* but not for *me*.

But holiness isn't just for saints and heroes. It doesn't mean being perfect or superhuman. Being holy means standing apart from the crowd, doing what's right even if you're doing it alone. It means doing little things with great love. It means actively growing in intimacy with Christ—even if that takes a lot of practice.

"You shall love the Lord, your God, with all your heart, with all your soul, and with all your mind."

Matthew 22:37

Our Call to Holiness

John was a gifted athlete; it just came naturally to him. But not for his younger brother, Tom. Tom was usually the last one picked when it was time to choose teams, and most of his game time was spent on the bench.

John knew Tom wanted to feel like an important part of the team. So he offered himself to Tom as his personal trainer. The brothers set up a regular backyard practice schedule. John worked diligently with Tom, helping him improve his skills and his attitude. Months passed, and everyone began noticing a new kid on the soccer field. Tom had confidence in himself. He had someone who believed in him—and he was finally in the game.

- *How would you define holiness?*
- *How were John's actions toward his brother holy?*

- *What does being holy mean to you?*
- *Who in your life comes to mind when you think of the word holy? Why?*

CCC 2012–16, 1691–98, 2028, 2427

Our Call to Holiness

- Read the introduction and answer the reflection questions together as a group. If you can, come up with a group definition of what it means to be "holy." Use this definition to answer the second reflection question.

- Finish reading the introduction as a group and give participants time to answer the next two reflection questions on their own.

- Discuss who participants chose as people they thought of as holy. List common personality traits and compare those words to your definition of holiness. See if there is any overlap. If there is, discuss why. If not, discuss why not.

We Are All Called to Holiness

- Ask participants why they didn't list themselves as holy people (if no one did). Ask them what they feel it would take for them to be listed as holy people.

- Give participants time to answer the reflection questions on their own.

Me? A Saint?

- Discuss with participants if they've ever felt called to become a saint.

- Create a list of actions, events, or personality traits participants think are required for becoming a saint.

- Give participants time to answer the reflection questions on their own.

- If you have time, ask participants what they do to work toward something they really want to achieve (*getting into their first choice college, making honor roll, getting a driver's license*). Then discuss how they can use that energy and desire to work toward becoming a saint, too. Emphasize that wanting to become a saint doesn't mean you have to give up all your other desires, it just means making sure those desires are oriented toward God and holiness *first* and not as an afterthought.

We Are All Called to Holiness

Both the Hebrew and Greek roots of the word *holiness* indicate a separateness, or a life that is set apart for God. As you work toward a holier life, your relationship with Christ will become even more personal. You will become less attached to the stuff of this world and more attached to what Jesus offers you in heaven.

What holiness looks like in the life of one person may not be what holiness looks like in your life. Just think about the variety of lives of the saints. One may be a contemplative nun, another a devout priest, and another the mother of five. Each of these lives would look very different, and the ways each of these saints lived holiness in their day to day lives would be very different, too.

Jesus is made visible in all of these lives, and each of these lives can become a light guiding others to holiness as well. Anyone who pursues goodness, truth, and beauty is seeking God, the source of these things. In each person's unique path to holiness, individual gifts and strengths play a large part.

But our holiness isn't based solely on the things we've done or the rewards and accomplishments we've earned. The source of our holiness, no matter what form it takes, is Christ who sanctified us.

- *Where do you see holiness in yourself?*
- *How can you nurture its growth?*

"'The Church on earth is endowed already with a sanctity that is real though imperfect.' In her members perfect holiness is something yet to be acquired: 'Strengthened by so many and such great means of salvation, all the faithful, whatever their condition or state—though each in his own way—are called by the Lord to that perfection of sanctity by which the Father himself is perfect.'"

CCC 825

Me? A Saint?

In the New Testament, the word *saint* is often a synonym for Christians. Because we, as Christians, are called to belong to Jesus Christ, we're called to be saints, set apart in holiness (see Romans 1:6–7). The saints recognized (canonized) by the Church took up this call to be set apart and lived it through the grace and mercy of God. They didn't become saints overnight. They had to work at it. Their lives of holiness took time, effort, and the desire to be as close to God as possible.

The saints grew in the same ways you are called to grow in your faith. They felt the call to holiness within themselves, and they wanted to live their lives in response to that call. They wanted it more than anything else. This desire to live like Jesus occupied their minds and influenced their decisions. This desire was the motivation behind all their daily activities. Whether big or small, every action was focused on God.

We aren't called to be more than human, but we are called to live our humanity as Jesus lived his. That's what sainthood is about, becoming fully human, becoming the person God created us to be.

"Strive...for that holiness without which no one will see the Lord."

Hebrews 12:14

- *Is there something in your life you want from the very depths of yourself?*
- *How is that desire oriented towards holiness?*
- *How can you align that desire with God's will?*

Keeping Holiness on Our Minds

"Woe to you, scribes and Pharisees, you hypocrites....on the outside you appear righteous, but inside you are filled with hypocrisy and evildoing."

Matthew 23:27–28

If we desire holiness like the saints, we need to keep God at the center of our actions and our thoughts. It's not enough for us to look holy on the outside if our inner thoughts and attitudes aren't filled with holiness. If our minds or attitudes are cluttered with feelings that don't lead us to holiness, or even lead us away from holiness, we'll have little room to grow.

We not only have to desire to become holy, we have to get rid of anything that stands in our way of holiness.

"If your right eye causes you to sin, tear it out and throw it away.... And if your right hand causes you to sin, cut it off and throw it away."

Matthew 5:29–30

- Name something that gets in the way of your desire for holiness.

Being a Christian, a saint, doesn't mean that goodness just comes to us out of nowhere. We still have to cultivate it, and our faith gives us the grace and guidelines we need to choose goodness and holiness. Sometimes this means we have to leave certain things, habits, and friends behind.

This doesn't mean those things, habits, or friends were evil (although some of our bad habits can be sinful), but it does mean that they were distractions keeping us from growing. Think about taking a trip. You have a particular destination in mind, and you want to get there. If you took every side road you saw, or stopped traveling and just stayed where you were, you'd never make it to your final destination. It's the same with holiness. If we stop moving toward it or allow distractions to pull us away, we'll never get there.

"Since we have these promises, beloved, let us cleanse ourselves from every defilement of flesh and spirit, making holiness perfect in the fear of God."

2 Corinthians 7:1

- What are some distractions that might keep you from holiness?

- What are some ways you can clear away these distractions?

The Quest for Holiness

Jesus didn't say holiness would be easy. Actually, he said it was so difficult some people might not even try for it.

"Enter through the narrow gate; for the gate is wide and the road broad that leads to destruction, and those who enter through it are many. How narrow the gate and constricted the road that leads to life. And those who find it are few."

Matthew 7:13–14

At first glance, this is discouraging. What's the use of trying for holiness if only a few people succeed in finding it? But there's another way to look at the "narrow gate": As a challenge we are all called to meet.

Somewhere within each of us is this narrow opening and the grace, given to us by the Holy Spirit, to enter through it. It might be hidden from us at first, but it's there. Finding it will be difficult. We will get hurt. We will get discouraged. We will have people tell us we can't do it or that the reward isn't worth it.

But through that narrow opening is the wholeness of life, the fullness of love, peace, and joy. We can have it. It's our birthright as children of God. We just have to desire it with all our hearts and be willing to work for it.

- In what way can the path to holiness be an adventure?

Keeping Holiness on Our Minds

- Discuss Matthew 5:29–30 as a group. Ask participants what they think this verse means for holiness? Emphasize that this verse shouldn't be taken literally but that God does ask us to cut those things out of our lives that cause us to sin. For example, if you know every time you hang out with a specific person you act in a way that isn't centered on God you don't just settle for "that's how it is." You stop spending time with that person and focus on recentering your life on God.

- Emphasize that this doesn't mean your friend, habit, or goal was evil necessarily. It just means it wasn't centered on God. After putting God first in your life you may discover you can experience that goal, habit, or person in a new way that *is* God-centered.

The Quest for Holiness

- Discuss the reflection question as a group, then move participants to working on the activity.

With a partner or on your own, think about the way to holiness as an adventure. What kinds of things would you need to bring with you? What people would you want by your side? Where would this adventure take you?

After you've thought about those questions, make a list, draw a picture, write a story, or anything else you think of, to show what your adventure toward holiness would look like.

With a partner or on your own, think about the way to holiness as an adventure. What kinds of things would you need to bring with you? What people would you want by your side? Where would this adventure take you?

After you've thought about those questions, make a list, draw a picture, write a story, or anything else you think of, to show what your adventure toward holiness would look like.

Think about your schedule for the upcoming week. What activities do you have coming up? What opportunities for holiness? Are there things you need to add or get rid of to help you keep holiness at the center of your life?

Journey of Faith for Teens: Mystagogy, M5 (826320)
Imprimi Potest: Stephen T. Rehrauer, CSsR, Provincial, Denver Province, the Redemptorists.
Imprimatur: "In accordance with CIC 827, permission to publish has been granted on July 12, 2016, by the Rev. Msgr. Mark S. Rivituso, Vicar General, Archdiocese of St. Louis. Permission to publish is an indication that nothing contrary to Church teaching is contained in this work. It does not imply any endorsement of the opinions expressed in the publication; nor is any liability assumed by this permission."
Journey of Faith for Teens © 2000, 2016 Liguori Publications, Liguori, MO 63057 All rights reserved. No part of this publication may be reproduced, distributed, stored, transmitted, or posted in any form by any means without prior written permission. To order, visit Liguori.org or call 800-325-9521. Liguori Publications, a nonprofit corporation, is an apostolate of the Redemptorists. To learn more about the Redemptorists, visit Redemptorists.com. Editors of 2016 edition: Theresa Nienaber and Pat Fosarelli, MD, DMin. Design: Lorena Mitre Jimenez. Images: Shutterstock.
Scripture texts in this work are taken from the *New American Bible*, revised edition © 2010, 1991, 1986, 1970 Confraternity of Christian Doctrine, Washington, D.C., and are used by permission of the copyright owner. All Rights Reserved. No part of the *New American Bible* may be reproduced in any form without permission in writing from the copyright owner. Excerpts from English translation of the *Catechism of the Catholic Church* for the United States of America © 1994 United States Catholic Conference, Inc.—*Libreria Editrice Vaticana*; English translation of the *Catechism of the Catholic Church*. Modifications from the *Editio Typica* © 1997 United States Catholic Conference, Inc.—*Libreria Editrice Vaticana*. Compliant with *The Roman Missal, Third Edition*.
Printed in the United States of America. 20 19 18 17 16 / 5 4 3 2 1. Third Edition.

Liguori PUBLICATIONS
A Redemptorist Ministry

Journaling

Think about your schedule for the upcoming week. What activities do you have coming up? What opportunities for holiness? Are there things you need to add or get rid of to help you keep holiness at the center of your life?

Closing Prayer

Ask for the intercession of the saints that we may one day join them before the throne of God. Then listen to the song you've chosen for this session. If music is unavailable, give participants time to reflect on holiness in silence and then pray the Lord's Prayer and Glory Be together.

Looking Ahead

As participants begin to think about holiness, ask them to also think about those good habits (or virtues) that make the path to holiness smoother. Let participants know you'll be talking about this more in your next session.

M6: Living the Virtues

Catechism: 1804–1829

Objectives

- Differentiate between the human and theological virtues.

- List the four human and three theological virtues.

- Recognize love (charity) as the greatest of the virtues.

Leader Meditation

Philippians 4:8–9

It isn't easy to live out the virtues in a world where people are prone to gossiping, to collecting a lot of material things, and to indulging in immediate self-gratification. We are called to a higher purpose. We were meant for something more. How do you live your life in Christ? Does your life conform to the world or does it seek to live out the virtues?

Leader Preparation

- Read the lesson, this lesson plan, the Scripture passage, and the *Catechism* sections.

- Find a recording of an Easter song to use for the closing prayer.

- Be familiar with the vocabulary terms for this lesson: virtues, human virtues, theological virtues. Definitions are provided in this guide's glossary.

Welcome

Greet neophytes as they arrive. Check for supplies and immediate needs. Solicit questions or comments about the previous sessions and/or share new information and findings. Begin promptly.

Opening Scripture

Philippians 4:8–9

Ask a volunteer to light the candle and read aloud. Think about our ultimate purpose: to be everything God meant for us to be. Before beginning your discussion of the lesson handout, discuss with participants *the similarities and differences of the life we are called to live (based on this Scripture passage) and the standard the world gives us for success.*

> "'[Virtue] allows the person not only to perform good acts, but to give the best of himself....The goal of a virtuous life is to become like God.'"
> CCC 1804

Journey of Faith

In Short:

- We see God's ways in the lives of those who practices the virtues.
- There are both human and theological virtues.
- The greatest of the virtues is love (charity).

Living the Virtues

We all have bad habits, sometimes we call them our "vices," but we rarely take time to think about our good habits, our "virtues." **Virtues** are those behaviors that make knowing what is good easy. They aren't merit badges that prove how good we are or how much more virtuous we are than someone else. They're ways of looking at and acting in life that shape us into the image and likeness of God.

> "[Virtue] allows the person not only to perform good acts, but to give the best of himself. The virtuous person tends toward the good with all his sensory and spiritual powers; he pursues the good and chooses it in concrete actions."
>
> *CCC 1768*

We have been given the special freedom to shape our lives in accordance with God's plan for us—or not. When we act virtuously we're cooperating with God's grace. Catholic teaching distinguishes virtues by two categories. Human virtues, also known as the moral or cardinal virtues, and theological virtues.

Human virtues, in cooperation with the daily graces given to us by God, are acquired through our own efforts, actions, and habits. They "govern our actions, order our passions, and guide our conduct" (CCC 1804). **Theological virtues** are a gift from God and are divine in origin. Both types of virtues help identify and define us as Christian disciples.

> - Do you think it's possible to live a truly Christian life with only one type of virtue? Why or why not?
> - How might human and theological virtues work together toward the same goal (living like Christ)?

The Human (Moral or Cardinal) Virtues

Prudence

Prudence guides the other virtues by setting boundaries and standards. It guides us to a right judgment. When we act with prudence we:

- examine the situation.
- compare all options and determine which one tends toward the greatest good.
- work to accomplish what has to be done.

Sometimes people mistake prudence for excessive caution or restraint. However, the prudent person is prepared to make the right decision when the time arrives. Prudence is judged not simply on whether the action produces some good (the ends) but also whether that choice (the means), is the best action tending toward the good.

CCC 1804–29

Living the Virtues

- Review the definition of *virtue* as presented in this section.
- Discuss the differences between human and theological virtues.
- Give participants time to answer the reflection questions on their own.

Prudence

- Discuss with participants how it can be bad to act without thinking or to act with extreme caution.

Suggested responses include: Acting without thinking can lead to us giving in to impulsive urges without taking the time to think about where that impulse came from and what the consequences might be. Acting with excessive caution or restraint may keep us from never stepping out of our comfort zones to do God's will or it can lead to consistent inaction.

- Then discuss how prudence finds a balance between these two extremes.

Suggested responses include: Prudence still requires us to act and accomplish things, but we act with all the facts and after examining the situation, consequences, and alternatives.

- Ask participants to come up with a scenario in which the virtue of prudence would be needed and why.

Justice

- Discuss with participants how it can be actually be unjust to act in a spirit of total equality without considering context, or payment based only on how many hours someone works.

Suggested responses include: People don't need the exact same things, and we need to consider the circumstances and needs of others as we discern the just action. People have different skills, abilities, and needs, and do different amounts or types of work that take varying amounts of time.

- Then discuss how justice finds a balance between these two extremes.

Suggested responses include: Justice allows us to get to know people as individuals. It allows us to think through a situation in context and consider the real needs of a person and his or her situation while discerning the just action.

- Ask participants to come up with a scenario in which the virtue of justice would be needed and why.

Fortitude

- Discuss with participants how allowing either self-doubt or fear of going against the group dictate our actions can keep us from doing God's will.

Suggested responses include: It's normal to be scared of trying something or to doubt whether we're good enough or prepared enough, but when we let those fears and doubts keep us from following through on God's call, we miss opportunities. No one wants to be an outsider, and standing up alone can be scary, but when we let public opinion tell us what to do we end up following the world's will instead of God's will.

- *What big decisions am I faced with? How can prudence help me make a decision?*

Justice

Justice is right action or right relationship. In this world, there will always be inequality, inconsistency, or disharmony among people. Perfect justice will come at the final judgment and only from God. However, the virtue of justice directs us to act with fairness toward God and our neighbor consistently and without hesitation.

When we act with justice we:

- consider the real (not just presumed) needs of others.
- take the situation into account before we act.
- take the time to get to know others as individuals.

Sometimes people think being just means giving everyone the same thing. But each individual has unique needs. For example, a parent has two children, one who needs glasses and one who has perfect, 20/20 vision. Is the parent being just by saying either both children get glasses or neither child gets glasses? Is the right action in this case different for each child?

When we act with justice, it is also important to remember Jesus' mercy. While payment and recognition based on merit is appropriate, think about the parable of the vineyard owner and workers (Matthew 20:1–16). He hired workers at various times in the day, but paid them all a full day's wages. While there is a "just wage," Jesus wants us to act not just with earthly justice, but with generosity which considers acts of compassion and mercy beyond what is simply the letter of the law.

- *Have you ever been in a situation where you needed something different than those around you (classmates, friends, siblings)?*

  Read the full parable of the workers (Matthew 20:1–16).

- *How would you feel if you had been working all day? Only a few hours? How do you see justice at work in this parable?*

Fortitude

Have you ever seen *The Wizard of Oz*? The Cowardly Lion's mission was to ask for courage. What he found on the way was a series of difficult and challenging situations where he had to forge ahead in the face of adversity. When he finally made it to Oz, he realized that he had become courageous on his own through his perseverance.

We act with fortitude when we:

- pursue good even when it's difficult.
- endure difficulties courageously and with purpose.
- continue to pursue good even when it requires sacrifice.

While prudence and justice guide our reasoning and choices, fortitude and temperance help us follow through. Fear or self-doubt may tempt us to abandon action. Peer pressure may sway us from choosing what is good. The person with fortitude will carry on.

- *Are you ever tempted to make decisions out of fear or pressure from others?*
- *How do you stand firm in your beliefs?*

Temperance

The key word for temperance is balance. Temperance counteracts the temptations of excessive pleasures and provides moderation in exercising our passions. It "ensures the will's mastery over instincts and keeps desires within the limits of what is honorable" (CCC 1809).

We act with temperance when we:

- carefully measure our use of created goods.
- measure, channel, and order our emotions toward good.
- eat and drink in moderation according to our needs.

Many people equate temperance with abstinence, but except in cases of addiction, where moderation isn't possible, that's not true. Temperance asks us to measure carefully our use of created goods, not

---

- Then discuss how fortitude can help us act even when faced with these fears.

Suggested responses include: You might not be an expert at it at first, but by following through you give yourself opportunities to get better and you build up your skills. By standing on your own, you show the world that your beliefs trump everything else, and you may even give someone else the courage to come stand with you.

- Ask participants to come up with a scenario in which the virtue of fortitude would be needed and why.

Temperance

- Discuss with participants how both excessive indulgence and excessive abstinence can be dangerous.

---

to avoid them entirely. A lack of balance often leads to consumerism, materialism, and amassing things while missing the deeper purpose of our lives.

Moderation or balance is especially important when we're dealing with emotions, which are critical in our moral lives. They spark the initial movement toward the good. Yet, they must be measured, channeled, and ordered toward the good continuously.

- *Is there something you struggle to moderate in your own life?*
- *What small step can you take toward tempering this habit?*

The Theological Virtues

> *"The theological virtues relate directly to God. They dispose Christians to live in a relationship with the Holy Trinity. They have the One and Triune God for their origin, motive, and object."*
>
> CCC 1812

The theological virtues originate in God, are effective under his direction, and have him as their destiny. Authentic human good and union with God go together. We can only find genuine happiness and fulfillment through union with the Triune God.

This union can't happen through our efforts alone, we will always find limits due to human frailty and sin. Faith, hope, and charity move us out of ourselves and help us grow in holiness.

Faith

Faith enables us to believe in God and in all he has revealed. It allows us to accept his presence and, more importantly, to fall in love with the God who first loved us.

Although faith is a gift, it must also be received and nurtured. No one becomes faith-filled by simply acknowledging God's existence or reciting a creed. Since faith is about friendship with God, it is sustained and strengthened in opportunities to get to know God. We can't become friends with someone we never spend time with. It's the same with faith. We can't grow in faith if we never let God into our lives. Faith comes in and through a community of believers—the Church.

There are two main outcomes of living with faith:

- *A good moral life.* We can't believe in God and not have concern for others. There's a necessary link between believing in God and right moral action.

- *A spirit of evangelization.* Consider how difficult it is to keep good news to yourself. Think of how excitedly we tell others about the things we love. Instinctively, we want to tell the whole world. We share good things because we want others to share our joy. The same is true for faith.

Faith nurtures a spirit of humility, gratitude, and determination to become who God has created us to be. It reminds us that God is greater than we are and always at work, even capable of bringing good out of evil. It frees us to bring about goodness in the world.

- *What impact has your relationship with God had on your life so far?*

Hope

> *"[Hope] keeps man from discouragement; it sustains him during times of abandonment; it opens up his heart in expectation of eternal beatitude. Buoyed up by hope, he is preserved from selfishness and led to the happiness that flows from charity."*
>
> CCC 1818

Hope comes from our confidence in God's presence and activity in our world. Hope means that we have a joyful longing for the coming of God's kingdom, when all the forces of evil will be banished. We don't wonder if God's kingdom will come, but when.

We see hope at work particularly in the expression of courage. Pursuing good in the face of adversity is difficult. Courage is grounded in the hope that God will bring to completion the good work begun in us.

- *How does your hope for God's kingdom give you courage as you live your faith?*

Faith

- Discuss with participants how faith can change our lives.

Suggested responses include: We live a life focused on others, we share and evangelize, we bring good to the world through God and the good news.

- Ask participants how they see faith influencing the human virtues discussed above.

Hope

- Discuss with participants how hope can change our lives.

Suggested responses include: We live a life oriented toward the promise of heaven, we have additional strength during struggles.

- Ask participants how they see hope being helpful for the human virtues discussed above.

Suggested responses include: God created us to be able to enjoy and find joy in things, but when we indulge in whatever we want whenever we want it we start to worship things and pleasures instead of God. Abstaining can, in some circumstances, be a good thing. However, when it's unbalanced it can become dangerous, as with anorexia. Any form of abstinence should be done with God first and center in our minds.

- Then discuss how temperance helps us find balance in our pleasures and passions.

Suggested responses include: Using temperance allows us to enjoy God's creation more. We can eat and enjoy delicious food without becoming unhealthy or ignoring the people with us at the table. We can enjoy the possessions we have without being controlled by the desire for more, and we can share easily.

- Ask participants to come up with a scenario in which the virtue of temperance would be needed and why.

Charity (Love)

- Discuss with participants how charity can change our lives.

Suggested responses include: We live a life focused on the love of God and others rather than ourselves, our accomplishments, or possessions.

- Ask participants how they see charity being necessary for the human virtues discussed above.

With a partner or on your own, list one way you see these virtues in action in the world and one way you can actively live them.

- Prudence
- Justice
- Fortitude
- Temperance
- Faith
- Hope
- Charity (Love)

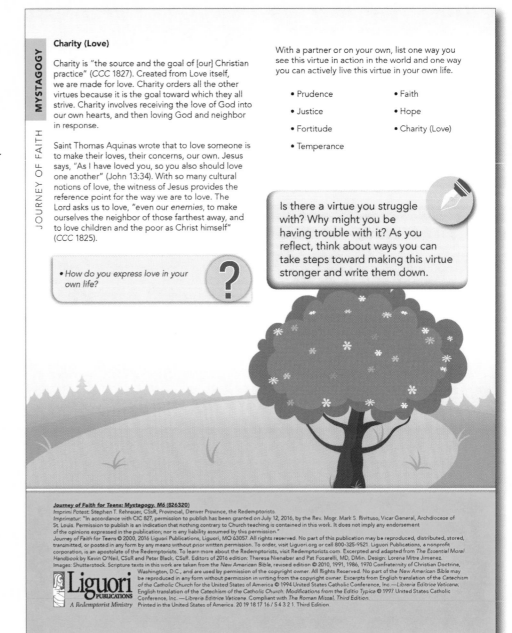

Charity (Love)

Charity is "the source and the goal of [our] Christian practice" (CCC 1827). Created from Love itself, we are made for love. Charity orders all the other virtues because it is the goal toward which they all strive. Charity involves receiving the love of God into our own hearts, and then loving God and neighbor in response.

Saint Thomas Aquinas wrote that to love someone is to make their loves, their concerns, our own. Jesus says, "As I have loved you, so you also should love one another" (John 13:34). With so many cultural notions of love, the witness of Jesus provides the reference point for the way we are to love. The Lord asks us to love, "even our *enemies*, to make ourselves the neighbor of those farthest away, and to love children and the poor as Christ himself" (CCC 1825).

- How do you express love in your own life?

With a partner or on your own, list one way you see this virtue in action in the world and one way you can actively live this virtue in your own life.

- Prudence
- Justice
- Fortitude
- Temperance
- Faith
- Hope
- Charity (Love)

Is there a virtue you struggle with? Why might you be having trouble with it? As you reflect, think about ways you can take steps toward making this virtue stronger and write them down.

Journey of Faith for Teens: Mystagogy. M6 (826320)
Imprimi Potest: Stephen T. Rehrauer, CSsR, Provincial, Denver Province, the Redemptorists.
Imprimatur: "In accordance with CIC 827, permission to publish has been granted on July 12, 2016, by the Rev. Msgr. Mark S. Rivituso, Vicar General, Archdiocese of St. Louis. Permission to publish is an indication that nothing contrary to Church teaching is contained in this work. It does not imply any endorsement of the opinions expressed in the publication; nor is any liability assumed by this permission."
Journey of Faith for Teens © 2000, 2016 Liguori Publications, Liguori, MO 63057. All rights reserved. No part of this publication may be reproduced, distributed, stored, transmitted, or posted in any form by any means without prior written permission. To order, visit Liguori.org or call 800-325-9521. Liguori Publications, a nonprofit corporation, is an apostolate of the Redemptorists. To learn more about the Redemptorists, visit Redemptorists.com. Excerpted and adapted from *The Essential Moral Handbook* by Kevin O'Neil, CSsR and Peter Black, CSsR. Editors of 2016 edition: Theresa Nienaber and Pat Fosarelli, MD, DMin. Design: Lorena Mitre Jimenez.
Images: Shutterstock. Scripture texts in this work are taken from the *New American Bible*, revised edition © 2010, 1991, 1986, 1970 Confraternity of Christian Doctrine, Washington, D.C., and are used by permission of the copyright owner. All Rights Reserved. No part of the *New American Bible* may be reproduced in any form without permission in writing from the copyright owner. Excerpts from English translation of the *Catechism of the Catholic Church for the United States of America* © 1994 United States Catholic Conference, Inc.—*Libreria Editrice Vaticana*; English translation of the *Catechism of the Catholic Church: Modifications from the Editio Typica* © 1997 United States Catholic Conference, Inc.—*Libreria Editrice Vaticana*. Compliant with *The Roman Missal, Third Edition*. Printed in the United States of America. 20 19 18 17 16 / 5 4 3 2 1. Third Edition.

Liguori PUBLICATIONS
A Redemptorist Ministry

Journaling

Is there a virtue you struggle with? Why might you be having trouble with it? As you reflect, think about ways you can take steps toward making this virtue stronger and write them down.

Closing Prayer

Gather as a group and play the closing song you've chosen for this session. If music is unavailable, pray the Lord's Prayer together.

Take-Home

Ask participants to actively look out for moments of virtue in their lives between now and the next session. They can record these moments in their prayer journal.

M7: Family Life

Catechism: 2201–13

Objectives

- Identify the family as the domestic church.

- Describe parents are the first and most important teachers of the faith.

- Recognize that faith and the Catholic identity is something to celebrate with family.

Leader Meditation

Colossians 3:12–21

Verses 12 through 17 of this passage help us to better understand the directives found in verses 18 through 21. Think about the relationships you have with the members of your own family, especially those involving teens. Pray for those virtues needed to make your home a place of warmth, peace, and love.

Leader Preparation

- Read the lesson, this lesson plan, the Scripture passage, and the *Catechism* sections.

- Find a recording of an Easter hymn or song used frequently in Masses at your parish.

- Bring stationery and envelopes.

Welcome

Greet neophytes as they arrive. Check for supplies and immediate needs. Solicit questions or comments about the previous sessions and/or share new information and findings. Begin promptly.

Opening Scripture

Colossians 3:12–21

Ask for a volunteer to light the candle and read out loud. You may prefer to use two readers—one for verses 12–17 and another for verses 18–21. Before beginning your discussion of the lesson handout, discuss with participants **the ways each family member can follow these directives in the name of love**.

"'The Christian family constitutes a specific revelation and realization of ecclesial communion, and for this reason it can and should be called a domestic church.' It is a community of faith, hope, and charity; it assumes singular importance in the Church, as is evident in the New Testament."
CCC 2204

Journey of Faith
of Faith

In Short:

- The family is the "domestic church."

- Parents are the first and most important teachers of faith.

- Faith, and the Catholic identity, is something to celebrate with family.

but we can influence our friends by living a life filled with deeper purpose and we can be an example to those who look up to us whether an underclassmen, younger sibling, or someone we don't even know is looking to us as an example.

- What can you do to make sure we build up our internal characteristics, and those of others, over earthly successes?

Family Life

Parents naturally want what's best for their children, just as we are called to want what's best for ourselves. Society's messages can lead us to think that fame, power, physical beauty, financial security, perfect health, success, wealth, and influence are what's "best" and most desirable. While each of these things has its perks, we likely see deeper and more lasting value in internal characteristics such as patience, kindness, goodness, generosity, self-respect, compassion, tolerance, integrity, and honesty.

It's our job as family members and mentors to be an example of these deeper, lasting gifts in action. Through our love, care, influence, and example, we help to strengthen the foundation of our family.

This is why the Catholic Church puts so much emphasis on the importance of family life. A happy and stable family provides the kind of atmosphere in which a child learns to relate to others: to care, to share, to love, to forgive. We don't just have this influence in our own family, although that may be where it's the strongest,

Faith and Our Parents

Our family is the place where we first learn about our ourselves and how to have relationships with others. These experiences form the basis of our self-image and begins our faith life.

"Parents have the first responsibility for the education of their children. They bear witness to this responsibility first by creating a home where tenderness, forgiveness, respect, fidelity, and disinterested service are the rule. The home is well suited for education in the virtues."

CCC 2223

Our parents are our first and most important teachers. We learn how to speak to others, to treat others, to cope with disagreements, to handle struggles, and to forgive all from the actions of our parents. As examples and teachers, our parents are never off duty, and as we grow up we realize more and more that our parents are like us—human and imperfect. Just like us, our parents make mistakes.

TEENS

CCC 2201–13

Family Life

- Ask participants to think about the kind of life their parents hope for them to have. They don't have to share (unless someone volunteers) or write their response down. Just ask them to hold on to this thought as you go through this session.

- As a group, answer the reflection question. If you have a board in your room, collect a list of ideas on it. If not, ask participants to write these ideas in their journal.

Faith and Our Parents

- Give participants time to answer the reflection question on their own. If you have time, ask participants to respond to this question by writing a letter to their parents. They don't have to share it if they don't want to. Let them know you have stationery and envelopes if they'd like to use them.

Faith and Our Family

- Discuss with participants how being compassionate and caring doesn't always mean letting someone act how they want. If it helps the discussion, shift the focus from parents and teens to teens and their friends (you wouldn't let your friend do something you knew would get them hurt or in trouble) or teens and teachers (the best teachers aren't the ones who let you turn in whatever you want but who help you make your work better).

- Ask participants to come up with several scenarios of times families might have disagreements. Then, as a group, come up with ways those disagreements can be solved using love and compassion rather than shouting.

- As you discuss these topics, be sensitive to participants who have unique or difficult family situations.

Living Faith With Family

- Go through each of the ideas here and ask participants *how* they think this activity will help their family grow in faith.

Suggested response include: When we make time to eat with each other we share in the same table fellowship Jesus shared with his disciples; we get to know each other better; we have the opportunity to learn from each other. When we pray together we bring God actively into our family life; we show we care about each other's faith. When we pray for our families we can take our frustrations and anger to God, learning how to react with compassion, etc.

MYSTAGOGY

JOURNEY OF FAITH

> - How have your parents influenced your faith? Is there anything about your faith you'd like to share with them?

> - Are there times you disagree or argue with your parents or other family members?
> - What's at the heart of these disagreements?
> - The next time you start to feel anger toward your parents or other family members, how can you respond with love and obedience instead?

Faith and Our Family

No one is perfect: not parents, not siblings, not cousins, not you. So family life is never perfect, either. Disagreements, arguments, sacrifice, compromise, and forgiveness are all elements of our family life. We can't just love our family members when things are good. Real love only exists when we forgive, understand, and accept each other despite our imperfections. God loves us unconditionally, under any and all conditions, and this is the kind of love we should strive for in our families.

> *"As long as a child lives at home with his parents, the child should obey his parents in all that they ask of him when it is for his good or that of the family....Children should also obey the reasonable directions of their teachers and all to whom their parents have entrusted them. But if a child is convinced in conscience that it would be morally wrong to obey a particular order, he must not do so."*
>
> CCC 2217

This doesn't mean our parents have to agree with, or even tolerate, our actions when we're behaving poorly or acting dangerously. Just as God sets guidelines and rules to keep us on the right path, our parents have a responsibility to set limits that keep us safe and teach us what's right and what's wrong.

Obeying our parents or guardians is an important element of our faith, so important the Fourth Commandment is to honor our parents. However, honoring our parents and our family doesn't just mean we obey. It means we participate in family life, especially our family faith life. We can become examples to our siblings and help our parents grow in faith.

Living Faith With Family

Not all families look the same, and no family is ever really "normal," let alone perfect. That's OK. Your family and your family life is unique to you, and there are a lot of ways you can bring your unique perspective on faith into your family.

The first step is making time to spend with your family. You're probably busy with schoolwork, extracurriculars, and maybe even a part-time job. Not to mention the time you want to spend on your own interests or out with friends. However, it's still important to spend quality time with your family, too.

Here are some ways you can work to spend more quality time with your family without sacrificing too much of your independence:

- *Eat dinner with your family as often as you can.* It can be easy to just grab food on your way to or from something else, but when you can, actually sit down and eat with all the members of your family. Put away or silence all the things that might distract you and give your attention to the people around you. Help prepare the meal or with cleaning up afterward, too.

- *Pray with your family.* Whether it's by leading grace before dinner, or asking your mom or dad to say a decade of the rosary with you in the car, you can share small moments of prayer with your family. If your family already has a set time for prayer,

---

- Answer the reflection questions as a group. Encourage participants to write down ways to share the faith with their family that appeal to them, and then actually try them at home.

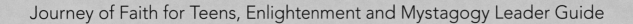

participate and take it seriously. You're an example for younger siblings, and your participation and input can make a big difference in how your parents experience prayer time, too.

- *Pray for your family.* If you can't get your family together for prayer, you can still pray for your family. Offer any special intentions up in prayer for the growth of your family. This can be an especially good strategy when you find your family members difficult to get along with. Instead of jumping into an argument, offer up your frustrations in prayer first.

- *Remember your extended family.* Our family is a lot more than just our parents and siblings. If you have extended family nearby, make time to visit them beyond just traditional holidays. Offer to drive your grandparents to Mass or to do chores around the house. If your extended family is far away, give them a call and keep in touch. Show them you care and let them know they're in your prayers.

- *Say thank you.* Your family does a lot for you. Let them know you notice the little things, like when your dad makes your favorite dinner or your sister helps wash dishes even though it was your turn.

- *Practice forgiveness and admit mistakes.* How do you feel when someone sincerely says, "I'm sorry" to you? How often do you say, "I'm sorry" to your family members? When live with people, they get on your nerves, they see you on your best and worst days and you see them on theirs. It's normal for arguments to come up. But the next time you feel yourself getting upset, take a step back and try to see things from a new perspective. Offer and ask for forgiveness as frequently as you can.

- What are some other ways you can share and grow your faith with your family?

Passing on the Faith

You're probably not thinking about starting a family of your own anytime soon. You may not want a family at all right now, or you may feel a stronger call to the religious life. If you do feel called to married life and to starting your own family, it's important to understand how much that decision entails.

In today's world, it's challenging to live and bring up a family within a Christian framework. The values of the consumer society are often at odds with the values of Jesus Christ. Living a Christian family life requires sacrifice, but the rewards of love, security, and a happy home will make it worthwhile.

> *"The home is the natural environment for initiating a human being into solidarity and communal responsibilities. Parents should teach children to avoid the compromising and degrading influences which threaten human societies."*
>
> *CCC 2224*

Should you become a parent, it will become your job to pass on the faith and make it relevant to your own children. The best way to do this is to build a strong faith foundation now, one that shows by example just what your faith means to you.

On your own, write a plan for how you'd like to see your family share in the experience of faith. Make sure it's something practical and do-able for your family. Share this plan when you get home and carry it out this week. Try to make it a routine your family gets into each week.

On your own, write up a plan for how you'd like to see your family share in the experience of faith. Make sure it's something practical and do-able for your family. Share this plan when you get home and carry it out this week. Try to make it a routine your family gets into each week.

Think about your own family.

- What are you grateful for?

- What do you struggle with?

- Is there a place in your family life for a stronger shared faith practice?

Journey of Faith for Teens: Mystagogy, M7 (826320)
Imprimi Potest: Stephen T. Rehrauer, CSsR, Provincial, Denver Province, the Redemptorists.
Imprimatur: "In accordance with CIC 827, permission to publish has been granted on July 12, 2016, by the Rev. Msgr. Mark S. Rivituso, Vicar General, Archdiocese of St. Louis. Permission to publish is an indication that nothing contrary to Church teaching is contained in this work. It does not imply any endorsement of the opinions expressed in the publication; nor is any liability assumed by this permission."
Journey of Faith for Teens © 2000, 2016 Liguori Publications, Liguori, MO 63057. All rights reserved. No part of this publication may be reproduced, distributed, stored, transmitted, or posted in any form by any means without prior written permission. To order, visit Liguori.org or call 800-325-9521. Liguori Publications, a nonprofit corporation, is an apostolate of the Redemptorists. To learn more about the Redemptorists, visit Redemptorists.com. Editors of 2016 edition: Theresa Nienaber and Pat Fosarelli, MD, DMin. Design: Lorena Mitre Jimenez. Images: Shutterstock.
Scripture texts in this work are taken from the *New American Bible, revised edition* © 2010, 1991, 1986, 1970 Confraternity of Christian Doctrine, Washington, D.C., and are used by permission of the copyright owner. All Rights Reserved. No part of the *New American Bible* may be reproduced in any form without permission in writing from the copyright owner. Excerpts from English translation of the *Catechism of the Catholic Church* for the United States of America © 1994 United States Catholic Conference, Inc.—Libreria Editrice Vaticana; English translation of the *Catechism of the Catholic Church: Modifications from the Editio Typica* © 1997 United States Catholic Conference, Inc.—Libreria Editrice Vaticana. Compliant with *The Roman Missal, Third Edition.*
Printed in the United States of America. 20 19 18 17 16 / 5 4 3 2 1. Third Edition.

Liguori PUBLICATIONS
A Redemptorist Ministry

Journaling

Think about your own family. What are you grateful for? What do you struggle with? Is there a place in your family life for a stronger shared faith practice?

Closing Prayer

Conclude with the song you've chosen for today's session. If music isn't available, pray a decade of the rosary together as family in the body of Christ.

Looking Ahead

Remind participants that while we are all part of different families, we also share in common one family in faith. As new Catholics, they are also called to grow their faith and share it with the world. Ask participants to think about ways they can do this kind of family faith sharing between now and the next session.

M8: Evangelization

Catechism: 429, 849–56, 901–13, 2471–74

Objectives

- Identify a relationship with Jesus as fundamental to conversion.

- Recognize that we are called to share the good news.

- Describe the ways in which the Church prepares and equips us for the mission of evangelization.

Leader Meditation

Reflect on the following excerpt from Matthew Kilmurry's *You Are the Catholic Brand:*

"You represent the Catholic Christian brand to everyone you meet. We often believe it's solely the responsibility of those living religious life. But in reality, the Catholic brand also belongs to lay Catholics who live, work, and play in the world outside the Church. You have been given tremendous power as a Catholic. Whether you know it or not, you are wielding that power at all times. There is no 'off' button. Your influence is always 'on' even if you don't feel like a good Catholic."

What Catholic brand do you show the world? How can you be more aware of the ways your actions influence others about the faith?

Leader Preparation

- Read the lesson, this lesson plan, the Scripture passage, and the *Catechism* sections.

- Be familiar with the vocabulary terms for this lesson: evangelization, witness. Definitions are provided in this guide's glossary.

- Extra Bibles and *Catechisms* for the activity.

- Meet with the hospitality team to organize light refreshments to celebrate the end of the formal RCIA process.

Welcome

Greet neophytes as they arrive. Check for supplies and immediate needs. Solicit questions or comments about the previous sessions and/or share new information and findings. Begin promptly.

Opening Reading

Invite a volunteer to light the candle and read the following excerpt from Matthew Kilmurry's *You Are the Catholic Brand:*

"A Brand Evangelist is someone so in love with a brand, a product, or a place that they do unofficial marketing for it. There's nothing more powerful for promotion. Who hasn't encountered a passionate fan of a movie, car, restaurant, or band? Their enthusiasm is contagious. Through that fan you live a transformational experience. All you need is the look on their face….This is true in our spiritual lives also. Those of us who are converts often feel unequipped to pass along the faith because we don't always know the details of our faith like the exact scripture quotes for a given situation or the accurate historical accounts. We are left paralyzed. But just as the Brand Evangelist doesn't know the ingredients of the pizza sauce or the car's suspension, we have to remember that all those details about the faith aren't the only thing people are attracted to. People are looking for an unforgettable experience. They're looking for conversion."

Before beginning your discussion of the lesson handout, ask participants **if they've ever been a fan of something they've loved so much they had to share it with everyone**.

> "It is from God's love for all men that the Church in every age receives both the obligation and the vigor of her missionary dynamism, 'for the love of Christ urges us on.'"
>
> CCC 851

Journey of Faith

In Short:

- A relationship with Jesus is fundamental to conversion.
- We are called to share the good news.
- The Church prepares us for the mission of evangelization.

- Who first introduced you to the Catholic faith?
- Why was their example so compelling?

Evangelization

"One day at lunch, a group of us started talking about religion. I started challenging Margaret, who was Catholic. I thought I knew what Catholics believed. Margaret very patiently explained what Catholic beliefs really are. Something about it stuck with me, and I decided I wanted to know more."

"I'd been going to a Catholic church for a couple of weeks but felt out of place so I just sat by myself. One day, a woman introduced herself and helped make me feel like I belonged."

"After my brother became Catholic, he sent me a lot of books by writers like Merton and Chesterton. I wasn't that interested, but as I started to read them I realized they made a lot of sense."

The Catholics in these anecdotes were evangelizing. In one way or another, they were witnessing and sharing the good news of the gospel of Jesus Christ.

Evangelization is something God calls all the baptized to do. As Pope Francis wrote in his apostolic exhortation The Joy of the Gospel (Evangelii Gaudium), "We know well that with Jesus life becomes richer and that with him it is easier to find meaning in everything. This is why we evangelize" (EG 266). Evangelization becomes part of us, part of who we are, so much so that we sometimes evangelize without even realizing we're doing it.

What is Evangelization?

Evangelization comes from the Greek word euangelizomai, which means "to bring or to announce the good news, the euangelion." When we evangelize, we're proclaiming the mystery of God's salvation of humanity in Jesus.

Evangelizing can mean the missionary work of bringing the gospel to people who've never heard the good news before. However, evangelization isn't limited to just this kind of mission. We can also evangelize by bringing the people around us, including other Christians, to a deeper awareness of Jesus Christ and his love. In fact, evangelization is the basis for all ministries within the Church because it equips those who hear the word of God to go out and live the word.

Evangelization has been important to the Church since its beginnings. Even Christ's last words to us before ascending into heaven were about evangelizing:

CCC 429, 849–56, 901–13, 2471–74

Evangelization

- Discuss with participants what influenced them to join the Catholic faith the most. If they only started RCIA initially because their parents wanted them to, ask what about the faith converted this into a decision they wanted to make for themselves.

- Give participants time to answer the reflection questions on their own, and then ask for volunteers to share.

What Is Evangelization?

- Give participants time to answer the reflection questions on their own.

- Then discuss the characteristics of the effective evangelizers participants have met. Keep, or encourage participants to keep, a list of these traits.

- Discuss how your participants plan to become evangelizers out in their own lives.

Step One:
Witness Christ

- Discuss what it means to be a witness with participants.

Suggested responses include: By living out the virtues, by staying informed about the faith, by living with faith at the center of our lives, by inviting friends to Mass or youth group meetings, etc.

Step Two:
Share Your Faith

- Make a list with participants of ways they can share their faith with their peers.

- Give students time to answer the reflection question on their own and then ask everyone to share at least one of these areas to create a group list. If you can, share commonly mentioned topics with your parish youth minister to aid in program planning for youth groups.

Step Three:
Offer the Option for Love

- Discuss with participants why evangelizing face to face might be more effective than evangelizing from a distance.

Suggested responses include: People can see and share in our enthusiasm for the faith, we can acknowledge better their dignity, etc.

"Go, therefore, and make disciples of all nations, baptizing them in the name of the Father, and of the Son, and of the holy Spirit, teaching them to observe all that I have commanded you."

Matthew 28:19–20

Someone's willingness to join the Church often has a lot to do with whether he or she already has a positive relationship with someone who is an active member. This example can make a crucial difference. That's why it's important for us to make our faith a public part of our lives, not just something we do in private.

- Who has been an evangelizer to you?

- How can you be that person to someone else?

How Do We Evangelize?

So now that you see how important evangelization is to faith, how do you get started? There are many ways to evangelize, but below is a five-step plan to get your started. This plan is based on the teachings of Pope Paul VI in his apostolic exhortation On Evangelization in the Modern World *(Evangelii Nuntiandi).*

Step One: Witness Christ

Jesus evangelized by proclaiming and witnessing the good news of God's love, justice, and mercy, and by sharing the hope of our salvation from sin and hopelessness.

Our first step in becoming a worthy evangelizer is to be a **witness**, to live our faith in Jesus Christ. Pope Paul VI pointed out that "Modern [people listen] more willingly to witnesses than to teachers, and if [they do] listen to teachers, it is because they are witnesses" *(EN 41).*

The positive witness of a loving, caring, and forgiving Catholic is the strongest method of attracting people to Jesus and to the Church. Our love leads others to Jesus Christ.

- How are you already a witness to the good news?

- How can you love more like Christ?

Step Two: Share Your Faith

The second step in evangelization is explaining the teachings of Christ in terms of what it means to be Catholic. Being a silent example for life in Christ isn't enough, "even the finest witness will prove ineffective in the long run if it is not explained, justified...and made explicit by a clear and unequivocal proclamation of the Lord Jesus" *(EN 22).*

Jesus didn't only live faith in God every day, he talked about what that faith and salvation meant for our daily lives. Jesus spoke with people about faith, he answered their questions and challenged them to live lives centered on God. His Sermon on the Mount, his parables, and his interactions with people show us how to share what we believe with others.

We can't dialogue about the faith well if we don't understand it. That's why the Church asks all those who are fully initiated into the Church to continue growing in faith. Many parishes offer youth groups that explore different areas of faith formation and provide opportunities to keep your spirituality fresh. The more you know about your faith, the more confident you'll be as an evangelizer.

- What are some areas of the faith you'd like to learn more about?

Step Three: Offer the Option for Love

This is the third step in evangelization; the reason we share our faith. Through evangelization we lead people to love in Christ. "To evangelize is to witness to God revealed in Jesus Christ, in the Spirit."

The best way to offer the option of love is person to person, face to face. People attract people. Love begets love. Love in action takes the shape of service. Even the simplest act of kindness can have a profound impact. The greatest act of kindness we can do for another is to offer them Christ's invitation of salvation from death and sin through a life of love, justice, and mercy.

- Who might you be called to evangelize to?

- How can you bring them the option for love?

EVANGELIZATION = LOVE

Pope Paul VI reminded us that to evangelize is to love. He noted three signs of love in the process of evangelization:

1. Respect for the religious and spiritual situations of those being evangelized. Our message of Christ's love shouldn't come through insults of another person's religion or spiritual beliefs. Debating with someone isn't a bad thing and can lead to strong conversion, but any disagreements should be handled respectfully and with knowledge of the situation and topic being discussed.

2. Concern not to wound the person, especially if that person is weak in faith. We are all in different places in our spiritual lives and we should present our faith as a space that offers forgiveness and mercy.

3. The effort to spread certainties anchored in the Word of God, not doubt and uncertainty because of our own lack of knowledge or improper study. This is why the call to continue our own education in the faith is so important.

Step Four: Challenge Our Culture

Our Catholic witness should affect the values of our society. Step four challenges us to be countercultural. Evangelization involves "affecting and...upsetting, through the power of the Gospel, mankind's criteria of judgment, determining values, points of interest, lines of thought, sources of inspiration and models of life, which are in contrast with the Word of God and the plan of salvation" (EN 19).

Jesus challenged hypocrisy, spoke against the powerful who took advantage of the poor, and condemned religious leaders who reduced the faith to minor practices and "neglected the weightier things of the law: judgment and mercy and fidelity" (Matthew 23:23).

Jesus asks us to do the same. We are called to bring the gospel to our society, to speak alongside the poor and homeless, to strengthen the place of marriage and family in our society, and to show respect for life. We can't do any of these things if we try to separate our religious life from life in our culture.

- Where do you feel called to bring the gospel in your life?

Step Five: Make the Good Better

The final step urges us to take what is positive in our society and put it at the service of the gospel. "Culture must be regenerated by an encounter with the gospel." This is our Christian responsibility. We must do what we can to see that advances in medicine are used at the service of life, and not to destroy it. We must work to make decisions that benefit the poor and abandoned in our global communities. We must sometimes sacrifice our own wants for the needs of others.

There is a lot of good in our culture, but that good can be made even better when touched by the transforming power of Christ's good news. We all still long for love, affection, and salvation. We still crave the good news of Jesus. That is why Vatican Council II said we should face the modern world with joy and hope, with the optimism of the life-giving gospel.

- What are some ways our culture supports the good?
- How can this good be made even better through an understanding of the good news?

Evangelize Ourselves First

When all is said and done, the first audience for evangelization is the active Catholic. Convinced Catholics will convince others. Caring Catholics will attract others. Our conversion is more than a once-in-a-lifetime event or the peak experience of being "born again." Evangelization is a process. Christ's call to build his Church must be offered again and again to Catholics through every stage of life.

Step Four:
Challenge Our Culture

- Make a list of ways our faith challenges our culture. Then ask participants to brainstorm ways we can effectively challenge these cultural norms.

Suggested responses include: Our culture is not always oriented toward life but promotes things like abortion as a "right" that improves the lives of women. We can go beyond protesting abortion to showcasing how other options, like adoption, actually improve the lives of multiple women and offer a life-filled alternative.

Step Five:
Make the Good Better

- List ways our culture already supports the good. Then list ways our faith can enhance these goods in society.

Suggested responses include: We already provide services for the poor or destitute, we can enhance them by not only providing material goods, but by providing them in a way that upholds the dignity of the person, providing for both their physical and spiritual needs.

On your own or with a group, create a list of questions you think others may have about the Catholic faith. Include questions you had about the faith before becoming Catholic. Pick one or two questions and research the answers. Use previous lesson handouts or your notes, the Bible, the *Catechism of the Catholic Church*, and any other resources you have access to. If you don't find an answer by the end of this session, keep searching.

On your own or with a group, create a list of questions you think others may have about the Catholic faith (include questions you had about the faith before becoming Catholic). Pick one or two questions and research the answers. Use previous lesson handouts or your notes, the Bible, the *Catechism of the Catholic Church*, and any other resources you have access to. If you don't find an answer by the end of this session, keep searching.

• How can you evangelize to the Catholics you know?

?

Describe one area of your life where you really could make a difference to others.

• How can you serve as an example of Christ?

Journey of Faith for Teens: Mystagogy. M8 (826320)
Imprimi Potest: Stephen T. Rehrauer, CSsR, Provincial, Denver Province, the Redemptorists.
Imprimatur: "In accordance with CIC 827, permission to publish has been granted on July 12, 2016, by the Rev. Msgr. Mark S. Rivituso, Vicar General, Archdiocese of St. Louis. Permission to publish is an indication that nothing contrary to Church teaching is contained in this work. It does not imply any endorsement of the opinions expressed in the publication; nor is any liability assumed by this permission."
Journey of Faith for Teens © 2000, 2016 Liguori Publications, Liguori, MO 63057. All rights reserved. No part of this publication may be reproduced, distributed, stored, transmitted, or posted in any form by any means without prior written permission. To order, visit Liguori.org or call 800-325-9521. Liguori Publications, a nonprofit corporation, is an apostolate of the Redemptorists. To learn more about the Redemptorists, visit Redemptorists.com. Editors of 2016 edition: Theresa Nienaber and Pat Fosarelli, MD, DMin. Design: Lorena Mitre Jimenez. Images: Shutterstock.
Scripture texts in this work are taken from the *New American Bible*, revised edition © 2010, 1991, 1986, 1970 Confraternity of Christian Doctrine, Washington, D.C., and are used by permission of the copyright owner. All Rights Reserved. No part of the *New American Bible* may be reproduced in any form without permission in writing from the copyright owner. Excerpts from English translation of the *Catechism of the Catholic Church* for the United States of America © 1994 United States Catholic Conference, Inc.—*Libreria Editrice Vaticana*, English translation of the *Catechism of the Catholic Church: Modifications from the Editio Typica* © 1997 United States Catholic Conference, Inc.—*Libreria Editrice Vaticana*.
Compliant with *The Roman Missal, Third Edition*.
Printed in the United States of America. 20 19 18 17 16 / 5 4 3 2 1. Third Edition.

Liguori
PUBLICATIONS
A Redemptorist Ministry

Journaling

Describe one area of your life where you really could make a difference to others. How can you serve as an example of Christ?

Closing Prayer

As this may be the last time you're all together as a group, ask participants to join hands in a circle. Remind everyone that our faith journeys continue far beyond this formal process. As a final prayer, go around the room and ask everyone to name one thing they are grateful to have learned our experienced through RCIA. After each, pray "thanks be to God."

Take-Home

Encourage participants to stay in touch with each other beyond these sessions and to support each other in living out the faith. If possible, celebrate with refreshments or dinner together.

Journey of Faith for Teens
Enlightenment and Mystagogy Glossary (alphabetical)

abstinence: Doing without (abstaining from) meat or another food or drink. Abstinence from meat is required only on the Fridays of Lent and Ash Wednesday, as determined by the American Catholic bishops.

apostolic: The Church "remains, through the successors of St. Peter and the other apostles, in communion of faith and life with her origin" (CCC 863). The Catholic Church is apostolic in three ways: (1) the Church is built on the foundation of the apostles (2) the Church hands on the teachings of the apostles with the help of the Holy Spirit (3) the Church continues to be guided and sanctified by the successors of the apostles, the college of bishops (CCC 857–865).

begotten: The doctrine God the Father caused God the Son to come into being before the beginning of time. Jesus was then born of the virgin Mary, Mother of God, but this birth did not diminish or alter his Godhood.

Book of the Elect: This book contains the names of those catechumens seeking enrollment in the Catholic Church. During the rite of election, catechumens will come forward and formally sign their names into the *Book of the Elect* as a way of expressing their desire for baptism. After catechumens have signed, they become the elect.

catholic: From the Greek word meaning "universal," in this context catholic describes the universality of the Church. The Church is intended for all human beings.

chrism Mass: Traditionally held in the morning before the official start of the Easter Triduum, during this Mass priests, together with their bishops, renew their commitment to priestly service, and the people are asked to pray for them.

common priesthood of the faithful: Through baptism, all Catholics have both the right and obligation to participate in this "common priesthood" of Christ. This priesthood calls for active and fully conscious participation in the liturgy (CCC 1141) including those particular ministries available to the laity, such as servers, lectors, cantors, and others (CCC 1143).

consubstantial: Used by the Council of Nicaea in 325, this word indicates that Christ is divine, "one in Being," of the same "substance" as God the Father. Christ is also consubstantial to humanity because he took flesh and "became like us in all things but sin" (Eucharistic Prayer IV).

conversion: From the Greek word *metanoia*, meaning "a profound and personal change." A conversion is more than just a change in the way things are done, but a true change of heart. In Catholicism, conversion means to turn away from sin and return to the love of the Father.

creed: An explanation or summary of the beliefs of the Church in the form of a profession of faith. The two most important creeds in Catholicism are the Apostles' Creed and the Nicene Creed.

discipleship: The act of being a disciple. Following Christ requires that we live truly Christian lives in word and deed, joyfully spread the good news, and actively participate in the sacraments.

evangelization: From a Greek word meaning "to announce," to spread the good news of the gospel, especially to those who have not yet heard, or would never otherwise hear, about Jesus Christ. In *Evangelii Nuntiandi*, Pope Paul VI writes, "Evangelizing means bringing the Good News into all the strata of humanity, and through its influence transforming humanity from within and making it new" (EN 18).

fasting: A traditional form of penance that requires the free choice to limit the kind or quantity of food or drink we imbibe. This is one way of sacrificing some good to God. Fasting, as required on Ash Wednesday and Good Friday, means to eat only one full meal during the day and only minor meals (such as bread and water) at other times during the day.

holy chrism: The sacred oil used in the sacraments of baptism, confirmation, and holy orders as well as during a church's consecration ceremony.

human virtues: Also known as moral or cardinal virtues, these are acquired through our own efforts, actions, and habits—always in cooperation with grace. They "govern our actions, order our passions, and guide our conduct" (CCC 1804). These virtues include: prudence, justice, fortitude, and temperance.

initial conversion: The first step toward lifelong conversion, this is the moment when we turn to Jesus Christ and accept him as our Lord and Savior, choosing to live a life of faith as a member of the body of Christ.

Mass of the Lord's Supper: This Mass is celebrated on the evening of Holy Thursday and marks the beginning of the Triduum. It is a celebration of the Lord's institution of the holy Eucharist. During this Mass, the celebrant washes the feet of twelve people in remembrance of the twelve apostles whose feet Jesus washed at the Last Supper. After this Mass, the Blessed Sacrament is taken from the main tabernacle to a smaller altar of repose.

mystagogy: A Greek word meaning "mystery," this is the final stage of the formal RCIA process. Taking place during the fifty days from Easter to Pentecost, its purpose is to help the newly initiated gain a deeper understanding of God's word, the sacraments, and what being a member of the Church means for their lives.

neophytes: In the context of the RCIA, those who have been "newly planted" in the faith through the sacrament of baptism.

oil of catechumens: The sacred oil used during baptism and during the period of the catechumenate.

oil of the infirm: The sacred oil used in the sacrament of anointing of the sick.

particular vocation: The vocation specific to us as individuals. We live out our particular vocation in our families, through our work, and as members of the community.

scrutinies: Three additional rites during the third, fourth, and fifth Sundays of Lent for the unbaptized elect. The purpose of these scrutinies is to examine one's life and to reflect on personal sin through the light of God's mercy and grace.

testimony: In the context of RCIA, this is a public statement from the catechumens and their sponsors on how the catechumens have chosen to respond to God's call. The catechumens affirm this testimony by signing their names in the *Book of the Elect* (see **Book of the Elect**).

theological virtues: These virtues originate in God, are effective under his direction, and have him as their destiny. "They dispose Christians to live in a relationship with the Holy Trinity. They have the One and Triune God for their origin, motive, and object" (*CCC* 1812). These virtues include: faith, hope, and charity (or love).

universal vocation: The vocation all Christians are called to live, which is a life of holiness as Jesus led.

virtue: A habit that makes it easier to know and to do what is good, shaping us more into the image and likeness of God (see **theological virtues** and **human virtues**).

witness: The act of a believer living out his or her faith in Jesus Christ, the gospel, and his Church through his or her thoughts, words, and deeds even when those actions result in personal sacrifice or the hostility of others.